Kingdom or Empire?

"This is an essential book for today. So many Christians have become confused about the gospel, and the resurging Christian nationalism is proof. The kingdom of God preached by Jesus was the antidote for power, coercion, and national pride. The gospel was the antidote for empire. This book reminds us that the good news is service, love of the stranger, and worship of Jesus alone as Lord. He alone is the one Word God has spoken, so we must trust and obey him, not nationalist visions to make any country great by Christian rule. And not the co-option of Christians with Christian symbols and language to give our loyalty to nationalist leaders as chosen by God."

—Tim Costello, Director, Ethical Voice Pty Ltd

"*Kingdom or Empire?* delivers a fast-moving theological analysis of issues often left to political scientists and commentators. In today's climate of polarization, Graham Joseph Hill challenges Christians to see the complexities of nationalism and populism through a biblical lens. His contrast between Christian nationalism and kingdom citizenship offers a compelling introductory framework for rethinking the role of faith in an age of upheaval."

—John A. Rees, Professor of Politics and International Relations, The University of Notre Dame Australia

"It feels like our world is teeming with little Caesars, each claiming sovereignty over their empires of dust, each appealing to the craven patriotism of their subjects. Their kind of populism bears no resemblance to the values of the reign of King Jesus. Thankfully, Graham Joseph Hill lays bare the stark differences between cheap nationalism and the good and beautiful kingdom of God. This is such a helpful book for our fraught times."

—Michael Frost, Director, Tinsley Institute, Morling College, Sydney

"In an age when the cross is so easily draped in the colors of the nation-state, Graham Hill offers a timely and prophetic call for the church to recover its primary allegiance to the kingdom of God. *Kingdom or Empire?* exposes the subtle ways Christian faith can be co-opted by projects of power, fear, and exclusion, and invites us back to the cruciform way of Jesus, marked by humility, justice, reconciliation, and love of enemy. Drawing wisely on Scripture, history, and contemporary global movements, Hill challenges believers to resist political idolatries without retreating from public life.

This is a courageous, clear-eyed, and deeply pastoral book that equips Christians to live faithfully as kingdom citizens in a contested political age."

—Michael P. Jensen, Rector, St. Mark's Anglican Church, Darling Point

Kingdom or Empire?

Following Jesus in an Age of Nationalism, Populism, and Political Idolatry

GRAHAM JOSEPH HILL

CASCADE *Books* • Eugene, Oregon

KINGDOM OR EMPIRE?
Following Jesus in an Age of Nationalism, Populism, and Political Idolatry

Cascade Books
An Imprint of Wipf and Stock Publishers
199 W. 8th Ave., Suite 3
Eugene, OR 97401

www.wipfandstock.com

PAPERBACK ISBN: 979-8-3852-6270-0
HARDCOVER ISBN: 979-8-3852-6271-7
EBOOK ISBN: 979-8-3852-6272-4

Cataloguing-in-Publication data:

Names: Hill, Graham Joseph, author.

Title: Kingdom or empire? : following jesus in an age of nationalism, populism, and political idolatry / Graham Joseph Hill.

Description: Eugene, OR : Cascade Books, 2026 | Includes bibliographical references.

Identifiers: ISBN 979-8-3852-6270-0 (paperback) | ISBN 979-8-3852-6271-7 (hardcover) | ISBN 979-8-3852-6272-4 (ebook)

Subjects: LCSH: Christianity and politics. | Nationalism—Religious aspects—Christianity.

Classification: BR516 .H54 2026 (print) | BR516 (ebook)

For Rick Lewis, my friend and spiritual mentor. Your unwavering faith, profound insights, and boundless compassion have been an endless source of inspiration. This work is a testament to the seeds you've sown in my spirit, helping me grow in ways I never imagined possible.

Contents

Introduction: When the Cross Is Captured

IN A WORLD CAUGHT between the tension of earthly empires and the reign of Christ, we must ask what it means to follow Jesus in an age increasingly defined by populism and Christian nationalism. As public leaders utilize religious symbols to enhance their political influence, the boundaries between faith and politics have become increasingly blurred.[1] But Christ's kingdom isn't of this world, and it doesn't draw its power from fear, division, control, manipulation, lies, or coercion.[2] Jesus Christ reveals his kingdom as one of love, justice, service, righteousness, humility, reconciliation, and truth, and his kingdom calls us to a different kind of allegiance: one that transcends the fleeting ideologies of nations and empires.[3]

The call to follow Jesus is to follow a radically different path that doesn't lead to domination but to the cross. Jesus invites us into the way of love, the truth of reconciliation, and the life of justice and mercy.[4] We don't need to participate in our time's culture wars and power struggles. Instead, our Creator invites us to live as Christ's faithful witnesses, offering a better vision for the world: one of peace, justice, hope, faith, and the boundless love of God.

CONTEXT OF THE CRISIS

Over the past few decades, we've witnessed a disturbing surge in nationalism and populist movements around the world.[5] Populism, and sometimes

1. Putnam and Campbell, *American Grace.*
2. John 18:36.
3. Bonhoeffer, *Cost of Discipleship.*
4. Matt 5:44; John 14:6.
5. Norris and Inglehart, *Cultural Backlash.*

its cousin, Christian nationalism, has grown in the United States, Europe (Hungary, Poland, Italy, France, Austria, Germany, and Sweden), Asia (Philippines, India, Myanmar, and Indonesia), Africa (South Africa, Kenya, and Nigeria), Latin America (Brazil, Mexico, and Argentina), as well as in Canada, Australia, Turkey, and Egypt. Populism often co-opts Christian and other religious language and symbols to serve political agendas.

Political leaders, hungry for power, have invoked "Christian values" to rally support, promising to return their nations to a perceived golden age of religious purity. But in doing so, they have conflated Christian identity with national identity, blurring the sacred and the political. This fusion of faith with populist rhetoric distorts the gospel of Jesus Christ, which calls us to transcend national borders and embrace the global vision of God's kingdom. What was meant to be a force for love and reconciliation has instead been twisted into a tool for division and exclusion.

For the church to reclaim its authentic witness, it must recover the distinctiveness of Christ's call. The way of Jesus can't be reduced to a political platform or national identity but is rooted in the eternal truth of God's reign over all humanity and creation.

Let me lay a foundation by defining the kingdom of God, empire, the spirituality of Jesus, the Jesus Way, populism, and Christian nationalism:

God's Kingdom: The reign of God, as revealed through Jesus Christ, is characterized by justice, peace, love, and reconciliation. Unlike earthly kingdoms, God's kingdom isn't built on power, coercion, or dominance but on self-giving love and humility. It invites all people into a community that transcends national, ethnic, and political divisions, where God's will is done on earth as in heaven. This kingdom is both a present reality and a future hope, calling believers to embody its values in the world.[6]

Empire: An empire is any political or cultural system that seeks power through fear, domination, and exclusion. Empires thrive on control, demand allegiance, and often distort faith to serve their ends. Empires promise security but demand compromise, especially of justice, humility, and truth.[7]

Spirituality of Jesus: Jesus's spirituality is a radical way of love, justice, righteousness, peace, humility, and self-giving service. It embodies the

6. Wright, *How God Became King*; McKnight, *Kingdom Conspiracy*; Ellul, *Presence of the Kingdom*.

7. Wright, *Paul and the Faithfulness of God*; Horsley, *Jesus and Empire*; Compier et al., *Empire and the Christian Tradition*.

kingdom of God: a reign not of coercion but of compassion, not of tribalism but of grace. Rooted in prayer, truth, and mercy, it calls us to live cross-shaped lives that subvert the values of empire and reflect the heart of Christ.[8]

Jesus Way: Acts 9:1–4 shows how the early Christians spoke about themselves as people of "the Way." What's the *Jesus Way*? Here's my definition: The Jesus Way is a life of radical discipleship to Christ, marked by love, grace, humility, justice, and communion with God and others. It means living the gospel daily, surrendering self-interest, embracing compassion, rejecting worldly power, and embodying peace, generosity, truth, and divine love.[9]

Political Populism: A political approach that emphasizes the division between "the people" and "the elite," often presenting a charismatic leader as the voice of the common person. Populism seeks to mobilize mass support by claiming that corrupt or out-of-touch elites are undermining the interests of ordinary people. It often appeals to emotions, simplifies complex issues, and promises to restore the people's power against perceived external or internal threats.[10]

Christian Nationalism: The belief that a nation should be defined and governed by Christian principles, with its identity, culture, and laws reflecting Christian values. It intertwines religious identity with national identity, asserting that the nation's moral and political life should align with Christianity, often at the expense of religious pluralism or secularism. It can involve using religious symbols and rhetoric to legitimize political power and exclusionary practices.[11]

Populism and Christian nationalism are distinct but often intertwined in modern politics. Populism focuses on championing "the people" against an elite, framing political struggles in terms of the common person versus a corrupt, out-of-touch ruling class. Christian nationalism, on the other hand, asserts that a nation should be defined and governed by Christian values, often using religious symbols and language to justify political power. These movements frequently overlap when populist leaders use Christian

8. Willard, *Divine Conspiracy*; Sobrino, *Jesus the Liberator*; Mulholland, *Invitation to a Journey*.

9. Hill, *Ten Movements of the Jesus Way*.

10. Mudde and Kaltwasser, *Populism*; Norris and Inglehart, *Cultural Backlash*; Müller, *What Is Populism?*

11. Whitehead and Perry, *Taking America Back for God*; Miller, *Religion of American Greatness*; Du Mez, *Jesus and John Wayne*.

imagery to rally support, claiming to defend a nation's Christian heritage or values. While populism appeals to the masses, Christian nationalism frames that appeal through the lens of religious identity and moral authority.

However, populism and Christian nationalism can be at odds with the kingdom and the way of Jesus. Jesus's kingdom isn't about power or domination but humility, justice, reconciliation, righteousness, service, and peace, transcending national borders and ethnic divisions.[12] Populism often fosters division and fear, while Christian nationalism can promote exclusion and identity-based power struggles. The kingdom of God, by contrast, calls for radical love, reconciliation, and service to others, including enemies. The values of God's kingdom challenge both populist rhetoric and the power-driven politics of Christian nationalism.

The intertwining of faith and politics isn't new, but its dangers have become alarmingly clear recently. We see crosses and Jesus banners waving at political rallies and even violent protests, such as the January 6 Capitol riot in the United States.[13] Religious symbols have been co-opted to advance political agendas, often promoting power, fear, and division.[14] This fusion of Christianity with political ideologies distorts the essence of the gospel and turns the church into a tool for power struggles rather than a witness to peace.

Jesus's message was love and humility, not domination or coercion. When faith is weaponized for political gain, it betrays the very teachings of Christ, whose kingdom wasn't one of force or fear but of compassion and reconciliation. It's a dangerous path to follow that distorts the integrity of the Christian witness and compromises the church's calling to stand as a countercultural force of peace and justice in the world.

God calls the church to be the body of Christ, a living witness to God's kingdom on earth. Yet, when Christianity is entangled with nationalism, this witness becomes distorted. The true message of Jesus, which is rooted in self-sacrifice, love, and justice, becomes diluted in favor of power, privilege, and exclusion. When faith is used as a justification for political power, it serves the empire rather than the kingdom.

This is precisely what happens when Christian nationalism aligns with the politics of fear and division. The church's prophetic voice, which

12. Phil 2:5–11; Matt 5:1–12.

13. Dias and Graham, "How White Evangelicals Fused with Trump Extremism"; Swanson, "Christian Nationalism."

14. Spencer, "Rise of Christian Populism" (2017).

is meant to call out injustice and advocate for the oppressed, is silenced or co-opted to serve the status quo. What was once a radical, countercultural movement becomes a tool for maintaining power and control. The church must ask itself: Are we reflecting Jesus's love and justice or the empire's values? To restore Christian witness, we must return to the heart of the gospel, which is about serving others, loving our enemies, reconciling peoples, promoting peace and compassion, and advocating for justice.

As the entanglement of faith and politics deepens, the church must engage in urgent self-reflection. The growing influence of nationalism and populism raises fundamental questions about the church's role in the world. How can Christians remain faithful to the gospel in a time when political ideologies are so often conflated with Christian identity? How can the church resist the pull of empire and stand firm in its commitment to God's kingdom?

In this book, I call for a recovery of Christ's spirituality, which transcends the political divides of our time and centers on the values of love, justice, and mercy. We must ask ourselves: In our actions, words, and allegiances, are we reflecting the heart of Christ, or are we allowing worldly ideologies to distort the message we're called to proclaim? The urgency of this moment calls for deep introspection, courageous repentance, and a reorientation of our lives around the eternal truth of God's kingdom.

To guide readers through this reorientation, each chapter of this book follows a ten-part structure:

- Two theological ideas
- Two historical case studies
- Two ethical and pastoral implications
- One individual spiritual practice
- One communal spiritual practice
- Two tools for cultural and political discernment

I've chosen this pattern to reflect the integrated nature of faithful Christian living: where deep theology, honest history, courageous ethics, grounded spirituality, and wise cultural engagement all converge. This structure ensures that each chapter transitions smoothly from reflection to action, offering readers both clarity and the courage to navigate an era of confusion, fear, and political idolatry.

KINGDOM VS. EMPIRE THEME

The kingdom of God, as proclaimed by Jesus, radically differs from the kingdoms of this world. While earthly empires operate by power, coercion, and fear, the kingdom of God is built on love, humility, and truth. Jesus's kingdom isn't of this world. God's kingdom doesn't rely on military might, political power, or coercive force. Instead, it's a reign of peace that breaks down the walls of hostility and brings together all peoples under the banner of God's love. Jesus called his followers to embody this kingdom, to be agents of peace and reconciliation in a fractured world.

The radical vision of the kingdom that Jesus proclaimed starkly contrasts the values of empire, which use force and fear to maintain control.[15] For the church, the challenge is clear: Will we align ourselves with the values of the empire, or will we follow Jesus in living out the radical vision of the kingdom?

The tension between the kingdom of God and the empires of this world is at the heart of this book's exploration. Jesus's kingdom isn't a political empire, nor do the divisions of nation-states bind it. Yet, the kingdoms of this world (whether populist or nationalist) often promise security, identity, and power to their citizens. These empires thrive on fear and exclusion, using the rhetoric of nationalism to draw lines between the "insiders" and the "outsiders."

In contrast, the kingdom of God is inclusive, calling all people (regardless of nationality, race, or status) into a new community defined by love, justice, and mercy. The church must navigate this tension, choosing to live out the kingdom's values, even when it's at odds with the demands of the empire. The question before us isn't whether we can peacefully coexist with the empire but whether we will remain faithful to the radical message of the kingdom.

To resist the distortions of nationalist ideologies, we must return to the spirituality of Jesus. This means reclaiming his teachings on servanthood, justice, peace, and mercy. Jesus's life and message show us that true greatness isn't found in power or dominance but in humble service to others. He taught us to love our enemies, to bless those who curse us, and to forgive those who wrong us. These teachings are the antidote to the seductive pull of empire, which promotes violence, retribution, and exclusion.

15. Wright, *How God Became King.*

In this book, I argue that the only way to counter the distortions of nationalism and populism is to recover the core values of Jesus's spirituality, which subvert the systems of power and violence that dominate our world. The church must embody these values in words and action, living out the radical love and justice that characterize God's kingdom.

The central dilemma Christians face today is whether to align themselves with the kingdom of God's or the empire's values. This choice isn't an easy one. Populism and nationalism offer promises of security, belonging, and power, but these promises come at a significant cost. They ask us to place our trust in earthly power systems rather than in the kingdom of God. The challenge isn't merely to choose between political parties but to decide where our ultimate allegiance lies. Will we serve the empire, or will we follow Jesus in embodying the values of his kingdom?

EARLY CHRISTIAN RESISTANCE TO EMPIRE

To understand what's at stake, we must begin where the church's confrontation with empire first took shape: under the shadow of Rome.

The early Christians lived under the oppressive weight of the Roman Empire: a vast system that demanded absolute loyalty, enforced emperor worship, and ruled through fear, violence, and the threat of punishment.[16] Rome's power wasn't just political but spiritual; it claimed the emperor as divine, and to reject this divine status was to threaten the very foundation of imperial rule. To follow Jesus in this world wasn't a mere personal or spiritual decision; it was a radical, countercultural act of resistance. When Christians declared "Jesus is Lord," they were proclaiming that Caesar isn't.[17] In that declaration, they laid bare the subversive nature of their faith, challenging not only the power of Rome but the entire structure of worldly authority. To the empire, such a declaration was treason, and many Christians (those who dared to speak this truth) paid for their faith with their lives.

The Roman slogan "Caesar is Lord" wasn't merely a political allegiance; it was a statement of divine supremacy. This loyalty to the emperor wasn't just about supporting a political regime; it was a religious act, a deep identification with the power of the empire. To refuse to honor Caesar in

16. Crossan, *God and Empire*.

17. Wright, *Paul*. Wright explores how "Jesus is Lord" functioned as a direct challenge to imperial ideology.

this way wasn't just to reject political rule; it was to defy the very idea that the emperor held divine status.[18] The empire demanded conformity to this belief, but the early Christians rejected it in a manner that defied Roman authority in its most sacred form. Refusing to burn incense to the emperor, for example, wasn't merely an act of civil disobedience but a declaration that their loyalty was, first and foremost, to Christ, not to the imperial system.

In this rejection, early Christians didn't resort to violence or rebellion; they resisted by embodying a different set of values altogether. They formed alternative communities: small outposts of hope, mercy, and justice that stood in stark contrast to the oppressive empire around them. These communities were places of care, compassion, and radical hospitality. They were places where the marginalized were not only welcomed but cared for: where the poor, the sick, and the strangers were valued and nurtured. Christians fed the hungry, rescued abandoned infants, and cared for the elderly and the oppressed.[19] Their commitment to each other was tangible, a fellowship that transcended boundaries of ethnicity, class, and social status. This was a subversive act. In a world built on divisions of power, wealth, and privilege, Christians chose to embody a kingdom where love was central, where justice flowed freely, and where grace and mercy prevailed.

Their worship wasn't merely a personal or private act but a profound political witness. When early Christians gathered to break bread, sing hymns, and share prayers, they were offering a counter-narrative to the empire's cult of power. Their very gathering was a statement: the empire's dominance couldn't erase the truth of God's reign. The table they shared was a place where the bonds of loyalty to the empire were broken, and in their place, a new vision emerged: a vision of a kingdom where the first would be last, where the meek would inherit the earth, and where the poor and oppressed would be honored.[20]

This alternative community wasn't a passive existence. It wasn't about disengaging from society but about radically transforming it through acts of love, service, and justice. The early Christians' refusal to bow to the emperor was a bold declaration of their allegiance to God's kingdom. But their resistance wasn't rooted in force or violence; it was rooted in the humility and servanthood of Christ, who did not come to be served but to serve.[21]

18. Hurtado, *Destroyer of the Gods.*

19. Stark, *Rise of Christianity.*

20. Acts 2:42–47 and Matt 5:3–12. For theological commentary: Hauerwas, *Matthew.*

21. Mark 10:45.

They understood that God's kingdom isn't advanced by coercion, military might, or political maneuvering but by humble, self-sacrificial love. In this way, the church became an alternative society that lived not according to the values of the empire but according to the principles of the gospel.

The early church's subversive stance continues to speak to us today. If Jesus is Lord, then no empire, no political system, and no earthly ruler can claim our ultimate allegiance. The empire's way (built on power, division, and violence) isn't our way. Instead, we're called to live according to the values of God's kingdom: justice, mercy, humility, and love. The early Christians embodied a kingdom that wasn't of this world, a kingdom whose power wasn't rooted in military might or political control but in the self-giving love of Christ. Their witness calls us to consider our allegiance. Are we, like the early church, living as a countercultural community, or have we allowed the values of empire to shape our lives?

This early Christian model of resistance (humble, nonviolent, reconciling, righteous, just, loving, merciful, generous, and courageous) is the foundation of every future act of kingdom resistance. It's a vision of a world where love triumphs over power, where justice rolls down like a mighty river, and where all are invited to live in the radical, transformative reign of God.[22]

As Christians, we must reexamine our loyalties, disentangle our faith from the day's political ideologies, and return to the radical, countercultural message of Jesus Christ. The choice we face is clear: the kingdom of God or the empire of this world.

NONPARTISAN, CHRIST-CENTERED, AND GLOBAL APPROACH

This book invites believers to rise above partisan loyalties and evaluate political movements through the lens of Christ's life and kingdom. Rather than endorsing any political ideology, it calls us to return to the centrality of Jesus, whose life challenges us to live with love, humility, and justice in a divided world.

I grew up in a right-wing, conservative setting and studied in a left-wing, progressive environment. I've seen the excesses of both groups. God's call to follow Jesus transcends all political ideologies. This book challenges both left-leaning and right-leaning Christians to examine where political

22. Amos 5:24.

allegiances have eclipsed loyalty to Christ. It encourages repentance, where politics has become an idol, distorting the gospel and hindering the church's mission to embody God's love.

This book speaks to both the peace-seeking and truth-telling aspects of the Christian faith with grace and truth. While it seeks to foster peace and understanding, it doesn't hesitate to confront the idolization of politics in the church. Christian conviction calls us to prophetic resistance, even as we engage with love and humility.[23]

This book calls Christians to evaluate all political movements by Jesus's standards: radical love for enemies, care for the oppressed, and a commitment to justice and peace. Politics must never supplant discipleship; our engagement with the world must reflect the kingdom's values, where reconciliation and mercy reign supreme.

While Christian nationalism in the United States is a significant concern, this book broadens the lens to a global perspective.[24] By examining how nationalism and populism shape Christian identity in different cultural contexts, we gain wisdom from experiences from across the world and learn how the church, across continents, responds to these complex challenges.

Case studies from history, such as the early church under Roman oppression and the Confessing Church in Nazi Germany, offer profound lessons.[25] These examples teach us how the church has resisted the temptation to intertwine faith with political power, preserving its integrity and prophetic witness even in hostile environments.

The struggles of Christians in apartheid South Africa and Latin America provide powerful examples of faith-driven resistance.[26] The church became a beacon of hope and courage in the face of political oppression, showing us that faith can be a force for justice and transformation, even in the darkest times.

Christians in China, thriving despite intense persecution, offer a remarkable testimony of the kingdom's resilience under oppressive regimes. Even in the face of the empire's attempts to suppress it, their unwavering faith reminds us that authentic Christian witness transcends political

23. Brueggemann, *Prophetic Imagination.*

24. Whitehead and Perry, *Taking America Back for God.*

25. Bonhoeffer, *Letters and Papers from Prison.*

26. De Gruchy, *Church Struggle in South Africa.*

borders, and our global community shares a common allegiance to Christ's reign.

TWO DISTORTIONS, ONE GOSPEL

In this book, I focus on the growing entanglement of Christian faith with nationalism and populism, particularly as seen in right-leaning contexts. This fusion often baptizes power, flags, and fear in the name of Jesus, trading the crucified Christ for a throne of political dominance. It distorts the gospel by making the church a servant of empire, replacing the kingdom of God with the nation-state's ambitions. The result is a discipleship shaped more by culture wars than by the Sermon on the Mount, more by fear of the other than by love of neighbor.

But this isn't the only distortion. While Christian nationalism often seduces from the right, there is an equally dangerous temptation on the left: a form of progressive syncretism and ideological accommodation. This emerges when the church loses its prophetic distinctiveness, trading costly discipleship for cultural relevance. In such a framework, the gospel is reduced to activism, holiness is seen as outdated, and doctrine is dismissed as exclusionary. The radical claims of Christ are softened to fit the moment, and the call to repentance is drowned in the language of affirmation.

Both errors (Christian nationalism and ideological accommodation) bend the gospel into the image of political ideologies. One clutches the sword; the other diffuses the cross into sentiment. One idolizes the nation; the other idolizes progress. Neither reflects the self-giving love, justice, and truth of Jesus.

So, if Christian nationalism deforms the gospel through *triumphalism and exclusion*, progressive syncretism can deform it through *accommodation and dilution.* Both replace Jesus as Lord with something else (nation, ideology, or culture) and both undermine discipleship in different ways.

This book begins by confronting Christian nationalism and right-wing populism. In future work, I'll turn to the distortions of the gospel found in progressive accommodation. Both are false gospels that demand our repentance, clarity, and courageous witness. Discipleship to Jesus means relinquishing the idolatries of both Christian nationalism and ideological accommodation and instead following the gospel and the way of Christ.

FOLLOWING JESUS, NOT POPULISM OR CHRISTIAN NATIONALISM

Jesus redefined greatness by showing us true power lies in humility and self-giving love. Unlike the self-serving narratives of populism and Christian nationalism, which often fuel division and elevate self-interest, Jesus calls his followers to embody sacrificial love. His kingdom isn't built on domination but on the gentle force of service. In a world that demands control and dominance, Jesus invites us to lower ourselves in love, care for the marginalized, and seek the good of others, even those who oppose us. The call of Christ isn't to rule but to serve.

Jesus, the Prince of Peace, embodies a truth that disrupts cycles of violence, division, and fear.[27] Nationalism and populism often seek to deepen these divides, using fear and exclusion as tools of power. But the truth Jesus brings reconciles all things. It's a truth that tears down the walls separating races, nations, and ideologies. In Christ, we find a radical unity that transcends the divisions created by empires and political ideologies. His call isn't to foster conflict but to offer peace, healing, and reconciliation to all, no matter their background.

The kingdom Jesus proclaimed is built on justice and mercy, not the ruthless pursuit of political power.[28] Populism and Christian nationalism often place control and dominance at the forefront, but Jesus's life teaches us that justice can't be separated from mercy. His ministry was a continuous call to stand with the oppressed, to uplift the poor, and to embody compassion. As his followers, we aren't called to hoard power but to share it, not to protect privilege but to challenge injustice. True discipleship means seeking justice with mercy and building a world where the broken are healed and the oppressed are lifted.

The gospel Jesus preached isn't a gospel of exclusion or division but radical inclusivity.[29] Christian nationalism, with its narrow definitions of who belongs, stands in direct opposition to Jesus's call to embrace all people. His kingdom is open to everyone, regardless of nationality, race, or background. Jesus broke every boundary the world sought to erect, from healing the outsider to breaking bread with sinners. His gospel is for everyone: the marginalized, oppressed, exploited, stranger, immigrant, friend,

27. Isa 9:6.

28. Matt 23:23; Mic 6:8.

29. Wright, *Mission of God*; Volf, *Exclusion and Embrace*.

fellow Christian, weak, powerful, wealthy, enemy, and those experiencing poverty. Christ's gospel calls us to love and serve all people as neighbors. The kingdom of God knows no borders, only love and welcome.

Let this truth settle within us: the Jesus Way is a path of radical love and a call to serve, heal, and reconcile, transcending all the barriers that human empires construct. Here, we find our true identity, which isn't defined by power or dominance but by the humble service of Christ, who leads us into peace, justice, and mercy.

1.

Kingdom or Empire?
Jesus's Vision in an Age of Political Power

As we step into the tension between the kingdom of God and the empires of this world, Christ invites us to reconsider our allegiance. Jesus's vision for the world stands in stark contrast to the power-driven narratives of nationalism and empire. He calls us to a life of love, justice, humility, and mercy that transcends all earthly power structures.

RECLAIMING THE KINGDOM AND SUBVERTING EMPIRE AND POWER

The term "kingdom" carries an inherent imperial connotation, often linked to domination and control. In a world burdened by oppressive monarchies, colonialism, and power imbalances, many believe that using "kingdom" perpetuates these associations, especially within contexts of ethno-nationalism or authoritarian rule.[1] Critics argue that "kingdom" distracts from the inclusive, radical love central to Jesus's message, making God's reign sound exclusive or militaristic. The metaphor, too often aligned with earthly power structures, risks implying that God's reign is yet another institution of hierarchical control. Furthermore, within cultures that value participation, community, and equality, the idea of a kingdom may feel out of touch with the countercultural essence of the gospel. Instead of a

1. For critiques of "kingdom" in colonial and nationalist settings, Rieger, *Jesus vs. Caesar.*

top-down, monarchical rule, some advocate for terms that reflect egalitarian values and the relationality of God's reign.

In response to the limitations of the term "kingdom," various alternative terms have emerged, each offering a richer and more inclusive vision of God's reign. The term "kin-dom," embraced particularly by feminist theologians (such as Catherine Keller), emphasizes a relational family of God, highlighting belonging and interconnectedness over hierarchical power structures.[2] Similarly, the "community of creation," proposed by thinkers such as Jürgen Moltmann and Elizabeth Johnson, focuses on the universal and cosmic scope of God's salvation, portraying the divine reign as encompassing all of creation.[3] The "Reign of God," popularized by Stanley Hauerwas and others, strips away political or colonial imagery, instead centering on God's sovereign rule.[4]

The "Beloved Community," made famous by Martin Luther King Jr., envisions a society built on justice, equality, and unconditional love: core values of God's kingdom that transcend divisive power structures.[5] The "Commonwealth of God" underscores mutual support, shared resources, and communal well-being, as articulated by N. T. Wright, and frames God's reign as one of flourishing and justice for all people.[6] "God's Justice and Peace," proposed by theologians like Dorothee Sölle, shifts the focus from dominion to active engagement in peace-building and right relationships, emphasizing fairness and reconciliation in the world.[7] Each of the alternatives seeks to invite more profound reflection on how God's reign transforms the world, fostering unity, justice, and love.

First Nations and Native American communities use terms that reflect a deep spiritual and relational connection to the land, ancestors, and all of creation, offering a worldview distinct from Western concepts of "kingdom"

2. Catherine Keller is often credited with developing and popularizing the term "kin-dom." Keller, *On the Mystery*.

3. Jürgen Moltmann and Elizabeth A. Johnson each articulate an ecological and cosmic vision of God's reign. Moltmann, *God in Creation*; Johnson, *Ask the Beasts*.

4. Stanley Hauerwas emphasized the "Reign of God" as a contrast to worldly power. Hauerwas, *Peaceable Kingdom*.

5. Martin Luther King Jr.'s concept of the "Beloved Community" appears frequently in his sermons and speeches. King Center, "Beloved Community."

6. N. T. Wright frames the "Commonwealth of God" in his discussions of justice and kingdom theology. Wright, *How God Became King*.

7. Dorothee Sölle links God's reign to justice and peace in her political theology. Sölle, *Silent Cry*.

or "empire." For many, the "Circle of Life" represents the cyclical, harmonious nature of existence, where life, death, and renewal are interconnected. The phrase "All My Relations" emphasizes the spiritual and ecological connections shared among all beings: humans, animals, plants, and ancestors.[8] The term "the Sacred Hoop" conveys the unity of creation, emphasizing a circular relationship rather than hierarchical systems. The concept of "Tiyospaye" (extended family) in Lakota culture stresses collective well-being, where each person belongs to a larger family rooted in shared responsibility. Terms like "Mother Earth" and "the Great Spirit" reflect a view of the divine that is immanent and relational, with the earth seen as sacred and deeply connected to spiritual life.

In Aboriginal and Torres Strait Islander theology, some theologians have proposed alternatives to the term "kingdom" that better reflect Indigenous worldviews and resist colonial associations. Anne Pattel-Gray, in *Through Aboriginal Eyes*, critiques the imperial overtones of "kingdom" and suggests that concepts like the Dreaming (which speak of relationality, land, ancestry, and spiritual belonging) offer a more holistic and just vision of God's reign.[9] Similarly, Garry Deverell, in *Gondwana Theology*, reframes Christian faith through Indigenous metaphors rooted in sacred Country and ancestral presence, challenging the dominance of hierarchical language.[10] Rather than "kingdom," these theologians evoke God's dreaming or creator's economy: terms that center community, land, and justice over domination and control.

These First Nations and Indigenous terms challenge the dominion-based models often found in Western traditions, emphasizing interconnectedness, stewardship, and unity over division and competition. They offer a vision of a world where all beings, regardless of their nature or origin, are respected and valued in a shared, divine relationship.

Despite valid concerns and the depth and richness that these alternatives bring to our fuller understanding of what Jesus was proclaiming when he spoke of God's kingdom, the term "kingdom" remains significant because it anchors Christian faith in the biblical narrative and Jesus's own words. The kingdom's centrality in Jesus's teaching presents a vision of redemption, justice, and peace rather than coercion or domination. Kingdom

8. For Native American theological expressions such as "All My Relations," see Woodley, *Shalom and the Community of Creation*.

9. Pattel-Gray, *Through Aboriginal Eyes*.

10. Deverell, *Gondwana Theology*.

evokes theological depth, tying God's sovereign rule to the fulfillment of divine promises, which include the restoration of all things. For Christians, it invites them into radical obedience and covenant relationship with God. I choose to continue using "kingdom" because it calls Christians to actively embody God's reign on earth, subverting earthly empires and kingdoms. It demands a reflection on the counter-imperial nature of God's rule, urging followers to live out justice and peace not just in words but through radical love. The term still retains the transformational power of Jesus's gospel.

Jesus's use of the term "kingdom" in the face of Roman occupation was subversive and prophetic precisely because it challenged the prevailing notions of empire.[11] In a world governed by brutality and power, he spoke of a kingdom not marked by domination but by justice, humility, and service. The kingdom he proclaimed was one of inclusion, reconciliation, and radical love, upending power dynamics. Jesus's kingdom was about freedom from oppression, especially for the marginalized, and his declaration was a direct contrast to the Roman Empire's oppression. His message was intentionally countercultural, making the "kingdom" a symbol of hope rather than tyranny. By using a term fraught with imperial weight, he subverted its meaning, demonstrating that God's reign isn't like the kingdoms of this world. Jesus's kingdom turned earthly power on its head, inviting all to experience the kingdom of peace and justice.

JESUS'S PROCLAMATION OF GOD'S KINGDOM AS AN ALTERNATIVE TO EMPIRE

In the face of empire, Jesus proclaimed the coming of God's kingdom. This proclamation was a revolutionary announcement that transcended the political and cultural systems of his time. The Roman Empire, with its legions of soldiers and oppressive rule, dominated the ancient world, asserting power through violence, fear, and exclusion. In stark contrast, Jesus's proclamation of the kingdom was an invitation into a new world order: a kingdom not of coercive power but of justice, mercy, humility, and service.[12] His message wasn't merely a call to spiritual renewal but a direct challenge to how human empires constructed their identities and authority. Jesus didn't present himself as another political leader seeking to overthrow

11. For a historical interpretation of Jesus's use of "kingdom" in the Roman context, see Horsley, *Jesus and Empire*.

12. Wright, *Jesus and the Victory of God*, 202–27.

the empire; instead, he revealed a kingdom that subverted the values of earthly dominions.

As N. T. Wright puts it, "The establishment of God's kingdom means the dethroning of the world's kingdoms, not in order to replace them with another one of basically the same sort (one that makes its way through superior force of arms), but in order to replace it with one whose power is the power of the servant and whose strength is the strength of love."[13]

When Jesus announced, "The time has come. The kingdom of God has come near. Repent and believe the good news!" (Mark 1:15), he was declaring that God's reign was breaking into the world in ways that would utterly transform how we understand power, leadership, and human flourishing. The kingdom Jesus preached wasn't one of military conquest or hierarchical dominance but one that welcomed the oppressed, the poor, and the meek (Matt 5:3–5). The "good news" Christ proclaimed was the arrival of God's justice and mercy for all people, not just the powerful or those in positions of societal privilege. The Sermon on the Mount (Matt 5–7) stands as the manifesto of this kingdom, where Jesus blesses the poor in spirit, those who mourn, and the peacemakers: values that stood in radical opposition to the Roman Empire's celebration of strength, wealth, and violence.

Jesus's refusal to advance his reign through violence is perhaps best illustrated in his conversation with Pilate during his trial. When Pilate asks Jesus, "Are you the king of the Jews?" (John 18:33), Jesus responds, "My kingdom isn't of this world. If it were, my servants would fight to prevent my arrest by the Jewish leaders. But now my kingdom is from another place" (John 18:36). Here, Jesus not only redefines kingship but also refuses to associate his kingdom with the worldly use of power. Unlike the Roman emperors who secured their thrones through military might and political maneuvering, Jesus demonstrates that the kingdom he brings is founded on self-giving love, humility, and the rejection of violence. His reign, though powerful in its transformative effects, doesn't operate by the world's standards of force and control.

This redefinition of kingship isn't just a theological abstraction but a call to action for all who would follow him. If Jesus's kingdom isn't of this world, then his followers are invited into a new way of living, one that refuses to conform to the violent, coercive power of earthly empires. The kingdom of God is about the restoration of relationships, the pursuit of justice for the oppressed, and the embodiment of mercy in a world that often

13. Wright, *How God Became King*, 201.

shows little of either. It's a kingdom where the first shall be last, and the last shall be first (Mark 10:31). It's the radical upside-down kingdom that invites us to challenge systems of power and to seek a world where the weak are made strong, the hungry are filled, and the broken are healed. Jesus's kingdom isn't of this world, and neither should the lives of his followers be.

EARLY CHRISTIANS' ALLEGIANCE TO CHRIST AS LORD OVER CAESAR

The early Christian community's bold confession that "Jesus is Lord" was more than a simple declaration of faith; it was a subversive, political act.[14] In the context of the Roman Empire, where loyalty to the emperor was paramount, the proclamation of Jesus as Lord was a direct challenge to the imperial system. The Roman Empire demanded absolute allegiance to Caesar, who was considered not only the ruler of the empire but also divine. The Roman slogan "Caesar is Lord" served as a reminder of the emperor's supreme authority, both politically and religiously. In this context, to confess "Jesus is Lord" was to openly reject the emperor's claim to ultimate power.[15]

This theological claim carried profound implications. Early Christians understood that their loyalty couldn't be divided between Jesus and Caesar. The declaration that "Jesus is Lord" meant that Christ, not Caesar, was their ultimate authority. This wasn't a mere spiritual assertion but a political one, as it fundamentally questioned the legitimacy of the empire's claim to rule. The refusal to participate in emperor worship, as seen in the martyrdom of Polycarp, revealed the depth of commitment early Christians had to Christ's lordship. When commanded to worship Caesar, Polycarp famously responded, "Eighty-six years I have served him, and he has done me no wrong. How then can I blaspheme my King and Savior?"[16] This refusal to worship the emperor, even at the cost of his life, was a profound declaration of allegiance to Christ's reign over all earthly powers.

For the early Christians, to say "Jesus is Lord" wasn't just an individual confession; it was a communal act that redefined their identity and mission in the world. It was an acknowledgment that Christ's kingdom, as proclaimed in the Gospels, wasn't of this world, yet it had the power to radically transform the world. In a society that viewed loyalty to the emperor

14. Horsley, *Jesus and Empire*, 145–53.

15. Reed, "Jesus Is Lord, Caesar Is Not."

16. *Martyrdom of Polycarp* 9.3, in *Apostolic Fathers*.

as essential to the well-being of the state, Christians stood firm in their allegiance to Christ, refusing to pledge their ultimate loyalty to any earthly power. In doing so, they became a countercultural movement that resisted the imperial system's demands for total allegiance and offered an alternative vision for the world founded on love, justice, mercy, and peace.

This allegiance to Christ wasn't passive. It demanded active resistance to the values and systems of empire. Early Christian writings and practices reveal a community that lived out its allegiance to Christ in tangible ways. They cared for the poor, stood up against injustice, and proclaimed the gospel of peace. They embodied the kingdom of God in a world dominated by the power of empire, showing that their true allegiance lay with the King who rules not through coercion and force but through sacrificial love.

The early Christians understood that if Jesus is Lord, then Caesar (and all the powers of the world) are not. This radical loyalty to Christ calls us to examine where our ultimate allegiance lies and how we're to live as witnesses to God's kingdom in a world that constantly seeks to align our faith with political and earthly powers.

JESUS'S TEMPTATION AND REFUSAL OF EARTHLY DOMINATION

The account of Jesus's temptation in the wilderness offers a profound insight into the nature of power and the way of the kingdom of God. As Satan offers Jesus "all the kingdoms of the world and their splendor" (Matt 4:8), he presents a seductive vision: a shortcut to power, a reign of earthly dominion without the need for suffering or sacrifice. The temptation is clear, compelling, and manipulative: seize control of the world and its systems, and all will be yours. Yet Jesus, in his wisdom, refuses this offer, choosing instead the path of the cross.[17] This moment isn't just a personal triumph but a pivotal teaching moment that reveals the radical nature of Christ's kingship and the rejection of worldly empire.

In choosing the way of the cross, Jesus demonstrates that his kingdom operates on entirely different principles than the empires of this world. Whereas empires expand through violence, coercion, and force, Jesus's reign is one of humility, servanthood, relinquishment, surrender to God, vulnerability, and sacrificial love. His rejection of the kingdoms of the world illustrates a fundamental truth: the kingdom of God isn't about domination

17. Wright, *How God Became King.*

or control. God doesn't advance the kingdom through military conquest, political maneuvering, or the accumulation of power: even though human empires and religious institutions often assume that this isn't just their way but also God's. It's a kingdom that grows through love, truth, justice, righteousness, service, humility, faith, hope, peace, and the profound transformation of hearts and minds. The cross becomes the ultimate symbol of this subversive reign: a kingdom that thrives not on the strength of armies but on the weakness and vulnerability of love.

This story isn't just about Jesus's rejection of worldly power, but it also serves as a cautionary tale for his followers. How often do we, like the disciples of old and many religious people in the present, flirt with the temptation of political power, believing that the way to advance God's work is through earthly dominion? In modern terms, the lure of political idolatry remains ever-present.

Many Christians today are seduced by the idea that national greatness or governmental control can be used to further God's kingdom, mistaking the power of empire for the power of Christ. But Jesus's response to Satan remains our guide. The path of Christ doesn't lead to political victories or national supremacy but to the humility of the cross. To follow Jesus is to reject the temptation of earthly dominion in favor of a kingdom that doesn't rely on force but on the power of love and sacrificial service.

The question we must wrestle with is this: Do we, in our hearts, long for the political power and national influence that the world offers, or do we genuinely seek the kingdom of God, a kingdom that subverts worldly systems of control? Jesus calls us to worship God alone and to serve him with a heart that isn't tainted by the lure of political idolatries. The kingdom of God isn't about conquering, controlling, or co-opting the world but about transforming it through the radical, otherworldly love of the cross.

THE EARLY CHURCH AS A COMMUNITY "IN" BUT NOT "OF" THE WORLD

The early church stands as a profound witness to what it means to live in the world without being shaped by its systems and values. In the second century, early Christians found themselves living in a world dominated by the Roman Empire. This regime demanded total allegiance from its citizens, including the religious worship of the emperor.

Yet, the early Christian community, despite living "in" the empire, remained steadfast in their commitment to the kingdom of God, refusing to bow to the demands of the empire. This tension is captured beautifully in the *Epistle to Diognetus*, which describes Christians as "sojourners" in their own land, citizens of heaven rather than of any earthly kingdom.[18] The letter marvels at the way Christians lived in their countries "but simply as sojourners," showing that their true allegiance wasn't to the emperor but to Christ.[19]

The early Christians' stance toward the empire wasn't one of rebellion but of radical difference. They lived as faithful citizens of earthly cities, paying taxes and contributing to society, yet they refused to acknowledge the emperor as a god. This refusal to worship the emperor was a direct challenge to the imperial claims of divinity and authority, as seen in the case of Polycarp, who was martyred for refusing to burn incense to Caesar.[20] For the early Christians, the confession "Jesus is Lord" was a political declaration, a rejection of the emperor's claim to ultimate authority. In this simple yet profound declaration, they made clear that their allegiance lay not with the empire but with the kingdom of God.

This refusal to align with the political powers of the day put the early Christians at odds with imperial expectations. The empire demanded loyalty, and in return, it promised security, stability, and honor. But for the early Christians, their loyalty to Christ meant that they couldn't give ultimate allegiance to any earthly power. Their citizenship in heaven redefined their relationship with the world around them. This radical loyalty to Christ often led to persecution, as Christians were seen as subversive and dangerous to the stability of the empire. Yet, their witness was powerful. They embodied the values of the kingdom (love, peace, humility, service, inclusion, and justice) in stark contrast to the values of empire, which were built on power, violence, and exclusion.

The early church, then, provides a model for us today. We're called to be "in" the world but not "of" it. This doesn't mean disengaging from society or withdrawing from political life; instead, it means that our ultimate allegiance must be to the kingdom of God. Our participation in the world must be shaped by the values of God's reign, not by the values of empire.

18. Halsted, "Quote: Epistle to Diognetus."

19. *Epistle to Diognetus* 5.1, in *Apostolic Fathers*.

20. *Martyrdom of Polycarp* 9, in *Apostolic Fathers*.

The early Christians demonstrate that living as citizens of heaven in a world dominated by empire means rejecting the claims of political power and instead embodying the radical love and justice of the kingdom. Their witness calls us to examine our own lives: Do we live in a way that demonstrates our allegiance to God's kingdom, or have we allowed ourselves to be co-opted by the empire's values of power, division, and control?

In a world still dominated by the forces of empire, the church is called to stand as an alternative society: a community that embodies the values of the kingdom. Just as the early Christians were "in" the world but not "of" it, so too are we called to live as faithful witnesses to the kingdom of God. Our loyalty to Christ must be our defining identity, and everything else (our nationality, race, ethnicity, gender, language, social status, nationality, politics, and ambitions) must be held in submission to Jesus Christ's reign.

NO EARTHLY NATION CAN BE EQUATED WITH GOD'S KINGDOM

The Bible presents a stark contrast between the values of earthly kingdoms and those of God's kingdom. Nations built on domination, conquest, and supremacy are never celebrated as models for God's people.[21] Instead, the Israelites are repeatedly called to a higher standard: one that isn't about national strength or political success but about humility, justice, and a radical service to others. This was as true for Israel's prophets in ancient times as it is for the church today.

Throughout history, many nations have attempted to equate themselves with God's kingdom, often in the name of divine destiny or righteousness. Ancient empires, such as Babylon and Rome, imposed their power through violence and coercion, claiming to represent the divine will.[22] In the modern era, nations such as Nazi Germany, Russia, Brazil, Hungary, Britain, and the United States, at times, have conflated nationalism with religious identity, believing that their political power somehow mirrored God's reign. These nations sought to use divine language to justify empire-building, imperialism, or exclusionary policies. Yet, their systems

21. For a theological exploration of how God's kingdom contrasts with worldly empires, see Wright, *How God Became King.*

22. For historical context on empires using divine justification, see Crossan, *God and Empire.*

(rooted in oppression, violence, and pride) have failed to reflect the justice, mercy, and love at the heart of God's kingdom.

Throughout Scripture, empires (whether the ancient Babylonian, Persian, or Roman powers) are consistently portrayed as failing to align with God's justice, and often, they actively oppose God's reign. No nation, regardless of its self-perception, can embody the radical inclusivity and peace of Christ's rule while pursuing dominance and division. Their failure lies in the fact that the kingdom of God can't be reduced to a political agenda or national identity; it transcends earthly power, calling us instead to love, serve, and reconcile.

In the face of nationalism and populism, believers must critically examine their hearts. Do we, as the church, allow the values of our political tribe or nation to supersede the commands of Christ to love, serve, and sacrifice? Is the success of our political movements more important than the global call to bring God's kingdom into being? The early Christians would have found any notion of "God's cause" being tied to the agenda of any one country to be utterly foreign. For them, Christ was Lord over all nations, and allegiance to him meant rejecting the imperial ideologies that sought to impose control through force and fear.

Christian churches must foster an atmosphere where God's global purposes take precedence over partisan triumphs. Congregations are called to be mindful of the language they use; they must avoid implying that God's work is tied to any specific national agenda or political party. Instead, we must strive to live as citizens of God's kingdom, transcending political divisions and remaining deeply committed to the values of love, reconciliation, and justice.

Christ's call isn't about disengaging from political life but about reshaping the way we engage, ensuring that our political involvement reflects Christ's teachings and doesn't compromise the integrity of his mission. The kingdom of God calls us to resist the temptation of national idolatry and to work toward a society that reflects God's justice for all people.

THE CHURCH AS AN ALTERNATIVE SOCIETY OF THE KINGDOM

Throughout history, many Christian communities have lived as alternative societies that embody the values of God's kingdom. The early church, refusing to bow to Roman imperialism, lived out a radical communal life, caring for the poor and marginalized, offering a profound witness to the world.[23] In the modern era, groups such as the Anabaptists, the Quakers, and liberation theologians in Latin America have embodied a kingdom-centered alternative, resisting violence, advocating for justice, and living simply.

These communities have shown the world what it looks like to live under Christ's reign, where love, peace, and reconciliation replace the world's quest for power and domination. Their witness calls the church today to embody the kingdom of God in ways that subvert worldly systems of greed, exclusion, and oppression.

The church, as the body of Christ, is called to be a tangible expression of God's kingdom in the world, an alternative society that lives out the radical values of love, mercy, and justice. If Christ's kingdom is truly our first loyalty, then the church must function as a contrast community within the broader culture. It isn't meant to mirror the power structures and social hierarchies of the world but to offer a vision of a radically different way of being: a community where Christ is King and all are equal under his reign. N. T. Wright powerfully describes the church as "the small working model of new creation," a visible sign of God's promise to redeem and restore all things.[24]

This theological vision calls us to embody kingdom values in our local congregations. The church should be a place where racial unity, economic sharing, and care for the vulnerable aren't only preached but practiced. These values preview God's future rule and serve as a witness to the world of what God's reign will look like. As believers, we're called to build communities that do not mirror the world's power plays and divisions but instead resist them by nurturing radical fellowship, where each person is valued equally and treated with dignity.

Pastorally, church leaders are called to nurture practices that actively resist imperial habits: those tendencies toward division, hierarchy, and the desire for dominance that characterize worldly systems. Instead of mirroring the patterns of the empire, the church must exemplify the new creation, where the dividing walls are torn down, and all are invited into the fellowship of Christ's love.

This kind of visible alternative community isn't about seeking political or social power; it's about demonstrating through our relationships and

23. For insights into the early church's communal practices, see Stark, *Rise of Christianity*.

24. McDade, "N.T. Wright"; Wright, "Early Christians and the Mission of God."

practices that Jesus's way is better. This is how the church proclaims to the world that the kingdom of God is here and now and that a new world is possible: not through power, violence, or domination, but through love, service, and justice.

The kingdom of God is a place where "there is neither Jew nor Greek, slave nor free, male nor female" (Gal 3:28). In Christ, these distinctions no longer define the worth or status of any person. The church, then, is meant to be a foretaste of this reality, a community where Christ's lordship reigns above all other allegiances and where his kingdom is lived out in the here and now. Through our shared life together, we become a living witness to the fact that God's rule is already at work in the world, drawing us together into a community of radical love and reconciliation that transcends all divisions.

PRAYING "THY KINGDOM COME" WITH REAL-LIFE IMPLICATIONS

The act of praying "Thy kingdom come, thy will be done on earth as it is in heaven" isn't just a spiritual exercise; it's a radical, subversive practice that realigns the heart with God's reign and dethrones the idols of power and self-interest that often grip our lives.[25] To pray these words is to invite God's justice, righteousness, love, mercy, hope, and peace to break into the world here and now. It's a prayer that calls us to surrender our anxieties, our desires for control, and our allegiance to worldly powers. With every utterance, we declare that God's will, not our own, should shape our lives and the world around us.

This prayer is deeply formational. It asks us to examine the ways we participate in systems of empire through pride, greed, ambition, fear, or the temptation to dominate.[26] Where do we align with the values of the kingdom, and where do we succumb to the spirit of empire, which seeks control, division, and exploitation?

Praying "thy kingdom come" calls us to an honest reckoning with these questions. It invites us to identify the places in our lives (personal, professional, or political) where we still seek to seize power and resist God's gentle rule. And it beckons us to yield these desires, consciously choosing God's sovereignty over the urge to grasp at worldly control.

25. Wright, *Lord and His Prayer*.

26. Brueggemann, *Prophetic Imagination*.

This prayer isn't simply a petition for the future; it's a daily practice that reshapes our priorities and our identity. When we pray, "Thy kingdom come," we aren't just waiting for a future event; we're aligning ourselves with the transformative work of God's kingdom in the here and now. It becomes a declaration of our deepest allegiance, not to a nation, a party, or an ideology, but to Christ, whose kingdom of justice, mercy, and reconciliation stands in glaring contrast to the ways of empire.

In this way, the Lord's Prayer becomes a personal "pledge of allegiance" to the radical, countercultural reign of Christ, helping us unlearn the ways of the world and embrace a kingdom that turns everything upside down.

CORPORATE WORSHIP THAT CENTERS GOD'S KINGDOM

The gathered church, in its worship and rituals, can and should function as a powerful countercultural witness to the kingdom of God. Corporate worship is more than a moment of individual reflection. Such worship is a communal declaration of our allegiance to Christ's kingdom and a means of reorienting our lives to his rule.

Through acts of worship, we rehearse the values of God's kingdom, embodying them in song, prayer, and Scripture, and thus fortifying our communal identity as citizens of a different realm. It's in these moments of gathering that we're invited to reflect on the sovereignty of God over all earthly powers and to remember that Christ is the true Lord, not any ruler or empire of this world.

One essential practice is to center God's sovereignty and justice in our worship. Singing hymns that declare God's reign over all creation and invoking God's justice in our prayers reminds us that we aren't mere subjects of the world's empires but participants in God's redemptive mission. Scripture readings, such as the exodus story or Mary's Magnificat, serve as powerful reminders that God's justice often stands in direct opposition to the values of the empire. Mary's song, for instance, proclaims that God "has scattered the proud in the imagination of their hearts" and "has brought down the powerful from their thrones" (Luke 1:51–52). These words speak not only of God's promises to Israel but of God's ongoing work in the world today: bringing down the idols of pride, greed, and power that dominate the earth.

Worship, then, becomes a formational practice that helps the church resist the pull of nationalism and empire. By regularly confessing "Jesus is Lord" in our creeds and songs, we actively fortify our hearts and minds against competing loyalties.[27] This confession challenges us to place Christ above any earthly allegiance, to reject the politics of division, and to embrace a global vision of God's kingdom.

As we pray for the global church and other nations during worship, we expand our hearts beyond our borders and national identities, affirming that the kingdom of God isn't confined to any one people but is a kingdom for all. Every time the church gathers, it has the opportunity to unlearn the myths of the empire and to embody the counter-formative truths of the kingdom. Through this corporate worship, we aren't simply waiting for a future kingdom to come; we're actively participating in the new creation, offering the world a glimpse of God's reign.

THE "SERMON ON THE MOUNT" LITMUS TEST

Amid the noise of modern political rhetoric, it's easy for Christians to be swept away by the loudest voices and most persuasive arguments, especially when those voices invoke moral language or appeal to religious identity. In such an environment, it becomes crucial for believers to have a discernment tool: a way to sift through the clamor and assess whether a particular movement or leader aligns with the values of God's kingdom or with the values of the empire.

Jesus provides us with a powerful litmus test: the Sermon on the Mount (Matt 5–7), a manifesto of the kingdom of God, offering a framework for understanding what true discipleship looks like in a world obsessed with power, pride, and fear.

In the Sermon on the Mount,

> Jesus delivers an astonishing vision of a new people who embrace a radical, world-transforming way of life in the world. This speech is a stunning description of Jesus's vision for life, discipleship, ethics, prayer, reconciliation, hospitality, justice, and community. It includes the Beatitudes and the Lord's Prayer, and it leaves his audience (ancient and modern) shocked and uneasy. Jesus calls his church to embrace a new, radical, ethical, and alternative way of life together in the world. He fulfills and reinterprets many aspects

27. Gorman, *Reading Revelation Responsibly*.

> of the old covenant and the Ten Commandments, and he soaks this vision in prayer, love, and grace.[28]

The Beatitudes themselves are a starting point for discerning whether a political movement or leader shows alignment with the values of God's kingdom or the empire: Blessed are the meek, for they will inherit the earth (Matt 5:5). Does the political agenda before us reflect meekness, or does it glorify arrogance and power? Blessed are the merciful, for they will be shown mercy (Matt 5:7). Does the message promote mercy or vengeance, showing compassion to the marginalized, or does it scapegoat others in the name of national interest?

By asking such questions, Christians can begin to discern where a political platform aligns with Jesus's values. The kingdom of God calls us to a radically different way of seeing the world: not one that seeks to conquer and divide, but one that seeks to heal, unify, empathize, reconcile, embrace, and restore.

The Sermon on the Mount provides a mirror to reflect the underlying values of any political platform or leader. Does the agenda seek reconciliation and peace, or does it stoke division and conflict? Does it elevate humility and self-sacrifice, or does it glorify pride and dominance? By holding the policies and rhetoric of political movements up to this mirror, Christians can more clearly discern whether they align with Christ's kingdom or the spirit of empire.

In an era of growing polarization, this simple but profound litmus test offers a way to filter out the noise of propaganda and return to the radical ethics of Jesus, whose kingdom isn't advanced through political power but through a cross-shaped love.[29]

ALLEGIANCE SELF-AUDIT AND "IDOL CHECK"

At the heart of the Christian life is the call to be wholly devoted to God's kingdom, not to any earthly power or political ideology. Yet, in a world where political allegiances often feel as sacred as faith itself, it's easy for believers to blur the lines between their commitment to Christ and their loyalty to their country, party, ideology, or political movement. To navigate this tension, a crucial spiritual practice is the "allegiance self-audit,"

28. Hill and Kim, *Healing Our Broken Humanity*, 152.

29. Phil 2:5–11; Mark 10:42–45.

a reflective exercise designed to help believers assess whether their patriotism or political engagement has become idolatrous.

The self-audit begins with a set of probing questions: Am I more emotionally upset by an insult to my country or party than by an insult to the character of Christ? This question cuts deep, asking us to examine whether our allegiance to national identity has surpassed our allegiance to Jesus, whose name and character should be the center of our hearts and lives.

Another question asks: Do I ever find myself compromising Christian ethics to achieve a political win? This question invites us to reflect on how often we overlook our calling to love, serve, and sacrifice in pursuit of political victories.

The most jarring of these questions is perhaps: Do biblical symbols (the cross, the scriptures) hold more sway over me, or do nationalist symbols (the flag, the constitution)? The cross of Christ stands as the supreme symbol of love and sacrifice, yet for many, national symbols may carry greater emotional and ideological weight.[30] This simple but powerful question invites a profound reflection on where our true allegiance lies.

The exercise goes beyond mere introspection; it serves as a practical means of identifying how empire-thinking (where loyalty to national or political powers becomes all-consuming) can subtly creep into our hearts. The Bible's warning is clear: You can't serve two masters (Matt 6:24). This is a stark reminder that Christ demands our ultimate loyalty.

The allegiance self-audit, when regularly practiced, helps Christians examine where political idolatry might be competing with God's reign in their lives. It isn't a call to disengage from the world's systems but to engage with a clear, single-minded devotion to Christ's kingdom. As believers conduct this audit, they open themselves to the transforming work of the Holy Spirit, ensuring that their devotion to the kingdom of God remains supreme, far surpassing any earthly empire or political allegiance.

Let's pause and reflect: Are we aligning ourselves with the kingdom of God or the fleeting powers of the world? This moment calls us to examine the loyalties of our hearts, recognizing that true allegiance lies not in the kingdoms of this world but in the reign of Christ, which beckons us to love, serve, and transform the world in his name.

30. 1 Cor 1:18; Gal 6:14.

2.

Christian Nationalism and the Seduction of Power

I'VE WATCHED CHRISTIAN NATIONALISM gain traction in Australia over recent decades: a troubling fusion of faith and flag. But it's not just here. In the United States, the rise has been evident, shaping politics, pulpit messages, and public life. Perhaps you've seen it in your community, too: when the cross is draped in a flag, and loyalty to Christ gets tangled with loyalty to country.

Christian nationalism offers a potent allure, one that promises the security of belonging, the strength of unity, and the sanctity of a nation consecrated by divine favor. Yet, this fusion of faith and nation comes at a cost: it distorts the very heart of the gospel.

Jesus Christ calls us to a kingdom that stretches beyond borders, flags, and the fleeting powers of any empire. The tension between allegiance to Christ's universal reign and the entanglement of faith with national identity demands a deeper, more discerning examination of how nationalism can become an idol, undermining the radical inclusivity and sacrificial love at the heart of the gospel, message, and example of our Lord Jesus Christ.

CHRISTIAN FAITH TRANSCENDS ALL NATIONAL BOUNDARIES

I define Christian nationalism as *the belief that a nation should be defined and governed by Christian principles, with its identity, culture, and laws reflecting Christian values. It intertwines religious identity with national identity, asserting that the nation's moral and political life should align with*

Christianity, often at the expense of religious pluralism or secularism. It can involve using religious symbols and rhetoric to legitimize political power and exclusionary practices.

The gospel of Jesus Christ isn't limited by borders, ethnicities, cultures, walls, or national identities: it's an invitation to all people, from every tribe, tongue, and nation, to experience the radical love of God. This message is central to the Christian faith, transcending all national boundaries. When Jesus commanded his followers to "make disciples of all nations" (Matt 28:19), he was commissioning them to spread the inclusive, all-encompassing reign of God, which sees no borders.

The kingdom of God is inherently transnational, a vision of unity that draws people together from every corner of the earth, welcoming all into a spiritual family of grace and peace. In the book of Revelation, we see this vision of a diverse, global community before God's throne: "a great multitude that no one could count, from every nation, tribe, people, and language" (Rev 7:9).

Christian nationalism, however, distorts this inclusive vision by elevating the identity of a single nation above the global church, creating an idol out of national identity. In doing so, it misrepresents the kingdom of God, attempting to reduce it to a mere extension of one nation's power or ideology. At its core, Christian nationalism places an earthly nation at the center of God's divine plan, misplacing Christ at the heart of the Christian faith. This error results in the idolization of national identity, where earthly citizenship takes precedence over the citizenship Christians hold in heaven (Phil 3:20).

The gospel, however, continually reminds us that our primary identity isn't defined by the nation to which we belong but by our identity as citizens of God's kingdom. No human borders or political systems bind this kingdom; Jesus builds his kingdom upon the eternal truths of love, justice, and mercy.

Thus, for Christians, any attempt to merge national identity with God's kingdom risks reducing the gospel to an ethnocentric ideology. The kingdom of God isn't about promoting any one nation's interests over others; it's about welcoming all into the family of God. Jesus modeled this radical inclusivity, calling his followers to embrace those on the margins, to love our neighbors (friends, family, strangers, foreigners, immigrants, and enemies) as ourselves, and to embody a love that knows no bounds.

The theology of Christian nationalism undermines these core values, shifting focus away from the global mission of the church and placing it instead on the fleeting powers of earthly empires. In contrast, authentic Christian faith calls believers to remain steadfast in their allegiance to the kingdom of God, which isn't of this world and does not depend on the power structures of earthly nations.

EXPOSING THE IDOLATRY IN CHRISTIAN NATIONALISM

Christian nationalism has subtly woven its way into the fabric of modern Christian identity, often under the guise of patriotism and faith. Yet, as we examine this phenomenon, it becomes clear that it represents a profound theological distortion. By blurring the lines between Christian identity and national identity, Christian nationalism creates a civil religion (a synthesis of faith and politics) that dangerously rivals the true faith of Jesus Christ. This ideology isn't historical, orthodox Christianity but rather a politically motivated movement that uses Christian imagery and language to justify national power, exclusion, and dominance.

David Swanson writes, "[Andrew L. Whitehead and Samuel L. Perry] have found three defining characteristics common among Christian nationalists. First, is the pursuit of power. For adherents of Christian Nationalism, the ends justify the means. The second is enforcement of boundaries. Christian nationalists, 'particularly if they are white, remain committed to the belief that real Americans (or at least "the good kind" of Americans) are native-born, white Christians.' Finally, Christian Nationalism seeks to maintain order in the public sphere by regulating private worlds such as gender roles and sexual norms."[1]

Christian nationalism often invokes the name of God, quoting Scripture and claiming divine blessing for a nation, while its gospel isn't one of repentance, salvation, and reconciliation but one of political power and cultural dominance. This selective appropriation of Christian teachings to advance political agendas represents a fundamental deviation from the message of Jesus.

Jesus taught that his kingdom isn't of this world (John 18:36). It's a kingdom built on humility, service, and sacrificial love, not one of coercion,

1. Swanson, "Christian Nationalism," quoting Whitehead and Perry, *Taking America Back for God.*

division, or domination. When nationalism becomes equated with Christian faith, it distorts the very essence of the gospel by suggesting that God's favor is reserved for a particular group or nation.[2] This idolatry is most apparent when national identity is elevated to the level of sacredness, as if God endorses a nation's political system, even when that system promotes exclusion or injustice.

The first commandment, "You shall have no other gods before Me" (Exod 20:3), reveals the idolatrous nature of Christian nationalism. By prioritizing national identity or political allegiance over God's reign, Christian nationalism places earthly systems of power and control above the divine calling to love, serve, and reconcile all people in Christ. It turns God into a tribal deity who favors one nation over another, disregarding the universal scope of God's redemptive plan.

The Bible consistently challenges this error, portraying worldly empires as broken and flawed while continually pointing toward God's global, inclusive kingdom. Theologically, Christian nationalism betrays the impartial nature of God, who desires to redeem all nations, not just one.

Theologically, Christian nationalism distorts the message of Jesus, substituting the radical grace of the gospel for the political agendas of empire. By elevating nation, ethnicity, or political tribe to sacred status, it distorts the very heart of the Christian faith, which calls us to seek God's kingdom above all else.

As Christians, we're called to a faith that refuses to bow to nationalist ideologies. Instead, we're summoned to embody the radical, inclusive love of God's kingdom, which transcends national boundaries, welcomes the marginalized, and challenges the unjust powers of the world. By returning to this Christ-centered faith, we find liberation from the idolatry of nationalism and are free to live out our calling as citizens of God's eternal kingdom.

CHRISTIAN NATIONALISM IN THE UNITED STATES

The United States, a nation shaped by its self-proclaimed Christian heritage, offers a striking case of how nationalism can intertwine with religious identity, producing a form of Christian nationalism that distorts the gospel.[3] This mindset has surfaced in various manifestations throughout the

2. Wright, *How God Became King*; Boyd, *Myth of a Christian Nation*.

3. Whitehead and Perry, *Taking America Back for God*.

history of the United States, but its presence has grown particularly strong in recent years. Nationalistic church services, where flags adorn sanctuaries and patriotic anthems are sung in place of traditional worship songs, have become all too common. Many are enthusiastic about fusing national and religious allegiances, identities, symbols, and practices. The blending of Christian symbols with nationalist slogans during political rallies (most notably seen in the January 6, 2021, Capitol insurrection) illustrates the extent to which the lines between Christianity and American nationalism have blurred.[4] Many US political and religious leaders stoke the flames of this religious-political-nationalistic synthesis, which distorts the gospel of Jesus Christ.

Research by sociologists Andrew Whitehead and Samuel Perry defines Christian nationalism as a cultural framework that merges Christian identity with American identity, seeking to preserve this union at all costs.[5] This dangerous fusion transforms the Christian faith into a political tool used to justify agendas that betray the very heart of the gospel. The message of Jesus is distorted for political and nationalistic ends as people grasp power, dominance, influence, and control.

Throughout history, the United States has witnessed the evolution of its civil religion, beginning with the concept of Manifest Destiny and the early rhetoric of American exceptionalism.[6] Phrases such as "In God We Trust" have subtly invoked divine approval for the nation's imperial ambitions, reinforcing the notion that the United States is uniquely chosen to fulfill God's will.

This framework, however, distorts the teachings of Christ, conflating the gospel's message of humility, service, and love with political power and national supremacy. For example, the Capitol insurrection saw individuals invoking prayers to Jesus and the cross to further a partisan agenda, a clear sign of how Christian symbolism is misused to sanctify political violence.

As Christian nationalism becomes more entrenched, the cross, which represents self-sacrifice and reconciliation, is wrapped in the flag, reducing the gospel's radical call to peace, reconciliation, repentance, hope, love, and justice into a tool for worldly power. This troubling trend begs the question: Can the church still be a witness to Christ's kingdom when its voice is entangled in the pursuit of earthly power?

4. Swanson, "Christian Nationalism." Also see Butler, *White Evangelical Racism*.

5. Whitehead and Perry, *Taking America Back for God*, 10.

6. Bellah, "Civil Religion in America," 1–21.

GLOBAL EXAMPLES OF CHURCH–NATION FUSION

While Christian nationalism is often associated with the United States, it's by no means a phenomenon limited to one nation. Around the globe, the fusion of church and state has manifested in various forms, each of which distorts the gospel by prioritizing nationalism over the kingdom of God.

In my country, Australia, Christian nationalism was used to justify the British invasion of these lands by framing colonization as a divine mandate to bring "civilization" and Christianity to Indigenous peoples. The doctrine of *terra nullius*, rooted in imperial and Christian assumptions, denied the sovereignty and humanity of Aboriginal and Torres Strait Islander peoples and nations.[7] Christian language and symbols were often employed to legitimize dispossession, mission settlements, removal of children from families, and cultural erasure, conflating national expansion with divine will.

In Russia, the Russian Orthodox Church has closely aligned itself with the state, with Patriarch Kirill playing a central role in justifying Russia's political ambitions, including its military actions, as a defense of Christian civilization.[8] Many Russian political and religious leaders justify the invasion of Ukraine through the fusion of religious and nationalistic language and ideas. The rhetoric used by Russian leaders echoes the very same principles of Christian nationalism, where the defense of the nation is framed as a divine mission. This blending of faith and politics not only undermines the integrity of the gospel but also creates a false dichotomy where loyalty to God and loyalty to the state become indistinguishable.

In Europe, countries such as Poland and Hungary have also adopted the concept of a "Christian nation," with leaders like Viktor Orbán emphasizing the importance of Christianity as a cornerstone of their national identity.[9] In these cases, political leaders use Christian language to justify anti-immigrant policies and resist multiculturalism, framing the struggle for national purity as a spiritual battle. This form of Christian nationalism exalts one ethnicity or culture above others, undermining the inclusivity and universal nature of the gospel. By positioning Christianity as a tool for preserving a particular national identity, these leaders distort the message

7. Harris, *One Blood.*

8. Luchenko, "Why the Russian Orthodox Church."

9. Fea, *Believe Me*, ch. 6; Main, *Rise of Illiberalism*; Spencer, "Rise of Christian Populism" (2017).

of Christ, whose kingdom welcomes all people regardless of nationality, ethnicity, or social status.

Looking to the past, the example of apartheid South Africa shows how Christian language was co-opted to support a deeply unjust system that claimed divine sanction for the racial segregation and oppression of Black South Africans.[10] Similarly, in twentieth-century Latin America, various political regimes used the church to legitimize their power by positioning themselves as protectors of Christian values against communism.[11]

In each case, the fusion of Christian identity with nationalist or political ideologies resulted in the distortion of the gospel's call to justice, peace, and reconciliation. These examples serve as a sobering reminder that whenever Christianity is harnessed to exalt one ethnicity, culture, or nation above others, it betrays the global, egalitarian nature of the gospel, which calls for the church to transcend all boundaries and embrace the unity found in Christ. When faith becomes a tool for political power, it ceases to be the radical, subversive witness it was meant to be. Instead, it becomes complicit in perpetuating systems of injustice and exclusion.

DISTORTION OF CHRISTIAN ETHICS AND WITNESS

Christian nationalism introduces a distortion to the core of Christian ethics, subtly replacing the gospel's call to love and humility with an ethic of domination and exclusion. Love your neighbor? No, dominate your neighbor. Welcome the stranger? No, fear and distrust the stranger. Care for immigrants and foreigners? No, reject and demonize them. Forgive your enemies? No, get retribution on your enemies so you can feel safe and secure. Christian nationalism manifests in a distorted form of patriotism, where the love that Jesus calls us to embody (radical, sacrificial, and unconditional) is replaced by the fear of "the other" and an unholy allegiance to the nation-state.

Jesus's life and teachings reveal that the path of discipleship is marked by self-giving love and a relentless pursuit of justice. Still, Christian nationalism often hijacks these sacred tenets, using them to justify exclusion and violence against those deemed outsiders. As Amanda Tyler poignantly writes, Christian nationalism is "a debasement of the most foundational teachings of Christ and Christianity—chiefly that we're all God's children

10. Villa-Vicencio, *Spirit of Freedom.*

11. Dussel, *History of the Church in Latin America.*

and that we should love each other as Jesus loved us, which was radically, sacrificially, and unconditionally."[12] Jesus calls us to love our neighbors, no matter their race, nationality, or creed. Christian nationalism's twisting of the gospel's message becomes a toxic force within the church, for when Christians bow to nationalist ideologies, they open themselves to excusing violence and oppression, even as "holy" acts performed in the name of their country.

Pastorally, the implications are stark. The church becomes a place where the exclusionary rhetoric of nationalism stifles the radical inclusivity of Christ. Fear replaces love, exclusion replaces embrace, domination replaces service, power replaces sacrifice, anger replaces mercy: and the list goes on. When the body of Christ is fractured along political and ethnic lines, the gospel loses its power to unite and transform. Communities, instead of being marked by mutual love and reconciliation, become arenas of division and suspicion. The church, once the harbinger of peace and justice, becomes complicit in perpetuating injustice by bowing to the idol of nationalism.

Churches that marginalize their members in the name of patriotism fail to see the image of God in those outside their political or national group. This exclusionary spirit stands in direct contradiction to the gospel that calls all people into a radical fellowship where boundaries of ethnicity, nationality, and status are erased in the light of God's love.[13]

The biblical call to see all people as God's image-bearers and to appreciate the divine presence in every person (especially those outside our circles) can't be overstated. The gospel is inherently global, and to tether it to a singular national identity is to betray the inclusive nature of Christ's reign. Christian nationalism fails because it doesn't reflect the kingdom of God, a kingdom built on mercy and reconciliation, not fear and division.[14] The church's prophetic witness to the world is compromised when we fail to embody the radical inclusivity that Jesus demonstrated.

12. Lagerwey, "How to End Christian Nationalism"; Tyler, *How to End Christian Nationalism*, 62.

13. Cf. Gal 3:28, which proclaims unity in Christ beyond ethnic, social, and gender boundaries.

14. Wright, *How God Became King*, which discusses the nature of God's kingdom as marked by mercy, justice, and peace.

THREATS TO DEMOCRACY, PEACE, AND CHURCH INTEGRITY

The dangerous alliance between faith and nationalism isn't just a theological error; it has profound political, ethical, and societal consequences. When faith is fused with nationalism, it shifts from being a force for justice and peace to a justification for domination and violence. The name of Jesus and the tools of religion are weaponized for the sake of nationalistic and other ideologies that oppose the gospel and love of Christ. The merging of religious zeal with nationalist fervor creates the perfect storm for justifying wars, oppressive policies, and deep-seated discrimination, all under the guise of divine righteousness.

The tragic history of religiously justified violence and the scapegoating of others is too long to ignore, and today's Christian nationalism is no different. In the United States, we witness how this ideology has contributed to a dangerous tolerance for authoritarian leadership and political violence. The January 6 Capitol insurrection, fueled by Christian nationalist rhetoric, is a grim example of how faith can be weaponized in pursuit of political power.[15] As sociologists have pointed out, Christian nationalism often leads to acts of intimidation and physical violence, with innocent people targeted in attacks on churches, mosques, temples, synagogues, and other spaces of worship.[16]

Pastorally, this intersection of faith and nationalism undermines the integrity of the church's mission. When the gospel is intertwined with a national agenda, the church loses its prophetic voice. Instead of calling for justice, mercy, and reconciliation, the church becomes an instrument of the state, offering blessings to policies and ideologies that contradict the very heart of the Christian faith.

This co-opting of the church to nationalistic agendas happened tragically in Nazi Germany, where the "German Christians" (*Deutsche Christen*) movement sought to align the church with the state's nationalistic and racist goals, reducing the gospel to a tool of political power.[17] The "German Christians" were a German protestant group that sought to align Christianity with the ideals of National Socialism, supporting Hitler's regime and

15. Whitehead and Perry, *Taking America Back for God*, 1–3; Du Mez, *Jesus and John Wayne*, 268–72, on Christian nationalism's influence on January 6.

16. Lagerwey, "How to End Christian Nationalism"; BJC and FFRF, "Christian Nationalism and the January 6, 2021 Insurrection."

17. Bergen, *Twisted Cross.*

church-state syncretism. When the church compromises its allegiance to Christ for the sake of national loyalty, it ceases to be the voice of the kingdom and becomes a chaplain to empire.

This isn't merely a political preference; it's a matter of preserving the integrity of the faith and the peace of society. When the church ties itself to nationalist agendas, it risks losing its credibility in the eyes of the world. Non-believers who see the church captured by nationalism may view Christianity as hypocritical, as the message of Christ is twisted to serve the interests of earthly empires. Therefore, resisting Christian nationalism isn't simply a matter of rejecting particular political preferences; it's about safeguarding the core message of the gospel and ensuring that the church remains a sanctuary of peace, justice, and reconciliation in a world increasingly torn by division.

CONFESSION AND REPENTANCE OF NATIONALISTIC IDOLATRY

Confession is healing for both the individual and collective soul and often serves as a turning point in people's lives. I know that when I confess sin, failure, posture, or attitude and dedicate myself to change, it feels like a burden has been lifted from my shoulders. The demands of change are real, but they sure feel better than the weight of shame, rebellion, guilt, and sin.

The journey of confession isn't merely a ritual but a profound invitation to return to the purity of Christ's call. Nationalism, often cloaked in the trappings of patriotism, can insidiously infiltrate our hearts, causing us to view our national identity as supreme.[18] It can blind us to the sacred truth that the kingdom of God transcends borders, cultures, nations, walls, and allegiances.

It doesn't matter whether these allegiances are conservative or progressive, Republican or Democratic, left-wing or right-wing, capitalist or socialist, for any political or nationalistic identity that elevates itself above the kingdom of God distorts the gospel and clouds our vision of Christ's universal reign. These allegiances, when left unchecked, divide and distract us from the radical unity and love to which Christ calls us. Thus, they require honest confession, heartfelt repentance, and a deep transformation of our priorities so that we might once again align ourselves with the countercultural values of God's kingdom.

18. Whitehead and Perry, *Taking America Back for God.*

To confess and repent isn't about condemnation but liberation. Confession is a chance to break free from the idols we've erected in place of the living God.[19] Repentance becomes a pathway to realign our hearts and minds with Christ's vision, allowing us to see beyond the narrow confines of nationalism and embrace a broader, more radical love for all people. In acknowledging how our allegiance to nation, ethnicity, or political ideologies has shaped us, we invite the Holy Spirit to uproot these deep-seated idols.

This practice of self-reflection creates space for God's transformative work to take root, cleansing us from the fear, division, and exclusion that nationalism often fosters. Through honest prayer, we open ourselves to a deeper intimacy with Christ, acknowledging where we have fallen short of living as citizens of God's kingdom.

Questions like, "Do I find more security in my nation's strength than in God's promises?" or "Have I allowed my political views to shape my Christian ethics?" serve as mirrors to the soul. These questions guide us toward the humility required for true repentance. When we confess these temptations to the Lord, we do not only admit to our failures, but we also release ourselves from the false gods of power, pride, and nationalism.[20]

The gospel calls us to a radically inclusive vision, and through repentance, we return to the heart of that mission, where the love of Christ is our ultimate allegiance, and all are invited into the embrace of God's family.

EMBRACING THE GLOBAL BODY OF CHRIST

In *World Christianity*, I write,

> Western churches, theologies, and missions aren't the future. We're a part of the future, as important as any other part of the global church. But we're not the future. The future of the global church exists in dynamic and global conversations. We need to move from a Eurocentric and Americentric view of mission and the church to one that prioritizes, respects, includes, and hears the whole global church. These conversations must be multivocal, multicultural, multi-peopled, missional, and glocal (global and local). They must involve people from the Majority World, First Nations, Indigenous cultures, and the West. The global church needs a thrilling

19. 1 John 1:9; Ezek 36:25–27.

20. Exod 20:3–5; Phil 2:5–11.

> glocal exchange. We need one characterized by mutuality, respect, partnership, and interdependence. Such exchange helps Majority World, First Nation, Indigenous, and Western churches learn from each other.[21]

As a community, the church is called to embody the radical inclusivity of God's kingdom. This kingdom breaks down barriers of race, nationality, and culture. To counteract the temptations of nationalism, we must cultivate practices that remind us of our universal calling as members of the global body of Christ. The church must be a place where the narrowness of national borders is continually widened, where the familiar is disrupted, and where the vision of God's kingdom is expanded.

One powerful way to do this is through the simple act of sharing in the community, as seen in practices like an "international night" potluck. In these gatherings, the food we eat, the stories we share, and the fellowship we experience help to dissolve the boundaries that nationalism seeks to create. As we sit at tables that are diverse in their expression, we participate in the vision of Rev 7:9, where every tribe, language, and nation stands united before the throne of God.

Another practice is global prayer. By intentionally praying for different countries each week or lifting up the needs of the global church, we train our hearts to see beyond our immediate contexts and recognize that the body of Christ is vast, varied, and beautiful. Praying in other languages, even with translations, serves as a tangible reminder that we're part of a living, dynamic global fellowship, not isolated to our individual nations.

Partnerships between churches across borders can further deepen our understanding as we walk together with our brothers and sisters in different parts of the world. Engaging in projects to support churches abroad or offering refuge to those fleeing oppression invites us to live out the gospel in ways that challenge the fear-driven isolationism of nationalism.

These communal practices aren't mere acts of charity but sacred disciplines that reshape our identity as a global people united in Christ. As we weep and rejoice with the worldwide church, we find that our allegiance to any one nation begins to fade, replaced by a deeper allegiance to the kingdom of God, where every person is a beloved child of the Creator, and all are welcome at the table.

Through such practices, we embody the hope that God's kingdom is coming here and now in every nation, tribe, and tongue.

21. Hill, *World Christianity*, 483.

PATRIOTISM VS. NATIONALISM: A DIAGNOSTIC GUIDE

When it comes to how Christians approach politics, it's crucial to distinguish between two often-confused concepts: patriotism and nationalism.[22]

Patriotism, when viewed through the lens of the gospel, is a deep and thoughtful love for one's country: one that isn't blind to its imperfections but strives to celebrate its virtues while working toward its betterment and the flourishing of its people. It's a love that remains humble, acknowledges the country's flaws, and seeks justice and reconciliation in alignment with Christian values. Patriotism holds the good of the nation in tension with love for all people, recognizing that our loyalty to our country should never diminish our duty to love our neighbors, especially those who are marginalized, oppressed, vulnerable, or from different nations.

Nationalism, however, is a more dangerous and idolatrous form of allegiance. It elevates one's nation to an uncritical, almost sacred status, demanding absolute loyalty and fostering an exclusivity that distances itself from others.[23] Nationalism thrives on the idea that one nation's interests must come before all others, and it frequently justifies dominance, exclusion, and even violence to maintain that superiority. This form of allegiance can quickly become a trap, where national identity becomes an idol that replaces God's call to justice, mercy, and the global fellowship of humanity. Nationalism turns a nation into a god: one that demands absolute devotion, often at the cost of compassion, equity, justice, empathy, and the moral teachings of Christ.

To navigate this dangerous territory, Christians must ask themselves tough, reflective questions: Are we able to love our country, acknowledge its flaws, and work for justice within it? Or do we unquestioningly defend it, closing our eyes to its wrongdoings? Do we see all people, regardless of nationality, as equals, or do we treat those outside our national borders with suspicion or disdain?

If the love of our country leads us to dismiss the dignity of others, to harm them for the sake of national pride, or to prioritize our nation over the well-being of the world, then it has become a form of idolatry. The question isn't whether to love our country but whether we're prepared to love it without allowing it to take God's rightful place in our hearts.

22. This distinction aligns with discussions in contemporary Christian ethics, emphasizing the importance of critical engagement with national identity.

23. For a theological critique of nationalism, see Volf, *Exclusion and Embrace*, 39–42.

Asking such questions about whether we've embraced patriotism or nationalism is a tool of discernment that helps us distinguish healthy patriotism from harmful nationalism. It invites us to hold our national pride in submission to the values of the kingdom of God and to regularly question our motivations. Christians can be good citizens without idolizing their country. By asking these deep questions, we're better equipped to live out a faith that transcends national boundaries, reflecting God's kingdom on earth as it is in heaven.

"NO KING BUT CHRIST" TEST IN POLITICS

The early church's bold declaration "No King but Christ" serves as a powerful guide for contemporary Christians navigating their political loyalties.[24] This motto speaks to the unyielding allegiance that Christ demands: not just as a spiritual leader but as the only true sovereign of our lives.

In our current climate, where political identities are increasingly intertwined with national identities, we must ask ourselves: Am I engaging in political discourse or making political decisions as if Jesus is my only King in this moment? The challenge here is to examine whether political loyalty (whether to a party, a leader, or a cause) has started to supersede the radical, transformative teachings of Jesus.

Every political claim, policy, and leader must be tested against the ethical framework of the kingdom of God.[25] Does supporting a political party or leader require me to compromise the values of love, truth, and justice that Christ teaches? When a political figure lies, manipulates, or mistreats others, do I excuse it for the sake of "my team," or do I hold them accountable to the standard of truth that Jesus sets? When a policy promises security but requires harm to the most vulnerable or dismisses the needs of people experiencing poverty, can I, in good conscience, support it? These are the questions that the "No King but Christ" test compels us to ask as we engage in the political process.

At the heart of this tool is the call to align every part of our lives (our actions, hearts, prayers, words, votes, empathies, services, and allegiances)

24. This phrase reflects the early Christians' refusal to acknowledge any earthly authority as supreme, emphasizing their allegiance to Christ alone. Wheelock, *Liberty of Conscience*, 29; O'Malley, "Under God."

25. This approach is consistent with the theological perspective that Christ's teachings should inform all aspects of a believer's life, including political engagement.

with the lordship of Jesus Christ. As Christians, we can't afford to let political narratives shape our faith; instead, our faith must shape our political engagement. The reality of Christ's reign demands that we scrutinize every political move, rhetoric, or agenda through the lens of the gospel.

If any movement or leader asks us to act in ways that contradict Christ's teachings (whether through hate, violence, dishonesty, fear, or division), we must reject it. In doing so, we assert that our ultimate allegiance is to Christ alone and that his kingdom, not the kingdoms of this world, is our true home.

The "No King but Christ" test, then, isn't simply a tool for making decisions; it's a practice that re-centers the believer on Christ's sovereignty, ensuring that no earthly power, no political party, and no leader can usurp his authority. By regularly examining our hearts and actions through this test, we maintain the integrity of our Christian witness, rejecting the subtle idolatry of political allegiance and instead embodying the countercultural values of the kingdom of God.

May we pause, then, and allow the Spirit of Jesus Christ to realign our hearts, where our loyalty to his reign transcends all earthly allegiances, and we find our true identity not in flags or nations but in the love that moves us toward compassion, justice, humility, and service, and binds us to one another in his name.

3.

Populism and the People of God

In a world where the voice of people is often louder than the voice of God, the challenge for Christians is to discern where true allegiance lies. When populism rises, promising simple answers to complex issues, it can be tempting to align ourselves with the crowd. However, Jesus calls us to a deeper, more discerning faith that listens not to the noise of the masses but to the subversive, countercultural, redemptive, and radically inclusive message of Christ's gospel and God's kingdom. These values (transformative, humble, self-sacrificial, peaceable, and reconciling) stand in stark contrast to the exclusionary, divisive, and often fear-driven rhetoric of populism.

SEEING GOD'S IMAGE IN ALL PEOPLE AND REJECTING "US VS. THEM"

I won't assume all readers are familiar with the term "populism." As the son of a truck driver, growing up in the working-class western suburbs of Sydney, I was often surrounded by populist rhetoric, but I wasn't acquainted with the concept. I define political populism as *a political approach that emphasizes the division between "the people" and "the elite," often presenting a charismatic leader as the voice of the common person. Populism seeks to mobilize mass support by claiming that corrupt or out-of-touch elites are undermining the interests of ordinary people. It often appeals to emotions, simplifies complex issues, and promises to restore the people's power against perceived external or internal threats.*

Populism thrives on division, often casting society into two opposing camps: "the righteous, good people" versus "the corrupt elites and dangerous others."[1] It capitalizes on a deeply ingrained fear of "the other," often pointing to immigrants, religious minorities, particular ethnicities, or those outside the majority culture as the source of societal ills. This binary thinking, which focuses on "us versus them," promotes an artificial division that undermines the unity and reconciliation God desires for all of creation.[2] In the face of such populist ideologies, Christians must return to the radical truth of the *imago Dei*: every person is made in God's likeness, worthy of dignity, respect, and love.

The doctrine of the *imago Dei* is a divine mandate to see each human being not through the lens of division but through the lens of unity and shared humanity. Whether rich or poor, migrant or native, citizen or outsider, believer or skeptic, powerful or marginalized, every person reflects the image of the Creator. This truth dismantles the boundaries that populism often seeks to reinforce and the "us vs. them" narrative that populism preaches, casting divisions between races, religions, political affiliations, and social classes. Populism thrives on such distinctions, using them as tools to cultivate fear and suspicion, but the gospel calls us to see beyond these labels and recognize the inherent dignity and worth in every human being.

Jesus broke down barriers of prejudice and division, especially with the parable of the good Samaritan (Luke 10:27–37), in which he upended ethnic and religious prejudices by presenting the Samaritan (a member of a group despised by the Jews) as the true neighbor. This radical reimagining of neighborliness calls Christians to love all people, even those whom populism demonizes or scapegoats.

The call of the gospel isn't to fear or exclude those who are different but to welcome them, to seek their welfare, and to see in them the image of God. As we read in Jer 29:7, God commands God's people to "seek the welfare of the city where I have sent you," regardless of who lives in that city. This principle should extend beyond borders, political ideologies, races, lifestyles, religions, and nationalities. For Christians, the gospel invites us to see the humanity in all people, rejecting the false divide that populism creates. Any ideology that encourages hatred, fear, suspicion, violence, or exclusion of a group of people is fundamentally incompatible with the way

1. Stooksberry, "Us-Versus-Them."

2. Coyne, "Populism and Religion."

of Christ. To follow Jesus means embracing the "other," not as a threat but as a fellow image-bearer of God.

RESISTING FALSE SAVIORS AND SIMPLISTIC ANSWERS

In the face of complex social, political, and economic challenges, populist movements present a dangerous allure: the promise of a simple solution to deeply rooted problems. Charismatic populist leaders often present themselves as the lone saviors of "the real people," fighting an apocalyptic battle against the so-called corrupt elites or dangerous others. In this dynamic, there is a profound temptation for Christians to place their messianic hope in a human leader or the collective will of the people rather than in God alone. This shift of trust isn't merely political; it's spiritual.

Populist ideologies promise to fix the world's problems quickly and decisively, often with slogans like "Just get rid of those people" or "If we take back control, everything will be better."

As I considered the simplistic promises and slogans made by populist leaders and parties, I recollected numerous examples. Populist slogans often capture the essence of a movement's appeal, simplifying complex issues into emotional rallying cries that resonate with the public. For example, the slogan "Make America Great Again" was famously used by Donald Trump during his 2016 presidential campaign, promising a return to a perceived past greatness.[3] In my country, Australia, populist slogans like "Stop the Boats" by Tony Abbott, "Put Australia First" by Pauline Hanson's One Nation, and "Jobs and Growth" used by Malcolm Turnbull in 2016 have often been employed to promote nationalism, tough stances on immigration, and economic security, simplifying complex issues into emotional appeals for political gain. In the UK, the Brexit movement adopted "Take Back Control," advocating for the country's sovereignty after leaving the European Union. In Hungary, Prime Minister Viktor Orbán has employed the slogan "Hungary First" to emphasize national pride and resistance to immigration. In Brazil, Jair Bolsonaro's "Brazil Above All, God Above Everyone" blended nationalism with religious sentiment, drawing strong support among conservative voters. Meanwhile, Italy's Lega Party championed the phrase "Italians First," focusing on anti-immigrant sentiment and national identity.

3. Wikipedia, "Make America Great Again."

These slogans often frame the "will of the people" against perceived elites, serving as a powerful tool for mobilizing populist sentiment.

But the gospel calls us to discernment and patience, recognizing that the root of evil isn't located in "them" (the outsiders or the opposition) but in the human heart itself. As the book of Proverbs teaches, wisdom is rooted in the fear of the Lord and the pursuit of truth, not in political expedience or simplistic answers. The gospel challenges Christians to resist easy solutions and to engage with the complexity of the world through the lens of Christ's love, justice, and peace.

The crowd mentality that populism often exploits is one of the most spiritually dangerous forces at work in modern politics. We see this reflected in the Gospels, where crowds could just as easily shout "Hosanna!" one day, only to demand "Crucify him!" the next (Matt 21:9, 27:22–23). The shifting sands of public opinion show how quickly the masses can be swept up by charismatic figures, only to be discarded when the tides change.

Jesus refused to be made into a populist hero (John 6:15), fleeing when the people wanted to crown him as their king by force.[4] His example teaches us a crucial lesson: our allegiance isn't to earthly powers or charismatic figures but to the kingdom of God, which transcends the fluctuating whims of populism.

In rejecting populist heroes and simplistic solutions, Christ Jesus calls his followers to maintain a deeper vision: one that seeks God's kingdom and righteousness above all else (Matt 6:33). This vision doesn't cater to base instincts or manipulate the fears of the masses, but instead offers a gospel that transforms hearts, restores justice, and builds a peace that passes all understanding. Jesus doesn't call us to be swept away by the current of popular opinion but to pay attention to the Spirit's steady, prophetic voice that calls the world to the more excellent way of Christ.

EUROPEAN "CHRISTIAN POPULISM" AND IDENTITY POLITICS

In contemporary Europe, populist movements have increasingly fused Christian identity with nationalistic rhetoric, aiming to secure power by appealing to a sense of religious and cultural purity. Politicians across the continent, from Italy's Lega Party to Hungary's Fidesz, have harnessed the language of "Christian heritage" to forge in-group identities, positioning

4. Osborne, "John 6:15."

their political platforms as defenders of Christianity against perceived threats such as Muslim immigration or secular liberalism.[5]

In these cases, Christianity is often reduced to a cultural marker, a tool to rally the masses, rather than a living, transformative faith. Symbols such as the crucifix or church imagery are wielded to solidify a national identity tied to Christianity, often overlooking the very teachings of Jesus: teachings rooted in love, mercy, and radical inclusion.

In Italy, the Lega Party capitalizes on fears surrounding immigration, positioning itself as the protector of Italy's "Christian roots" against the influx of Muslims. Similarly, Hungary's Prime Minister Viktor Orbán has linked his political agenda to the defense of Christianity, positioning Hungary as a bastion of Christian values in Europe.[6] However, these nationalist movements betray the gospel they claim to protect by prioritizing ethnic identity over the inclusive call of Christ.

As scholars have pointed out, these parties often invoke the language of "Christendom," emphasizing the idea of a Christian civilization, but their policies (like rejecting refugees or promoting exclusionary laws) stand in direct contradiction to the core teachings of Christ. This distorting of Christianity into "Christianism," as it has been termed, isn't only a betrayal of the gospel but also a corruption of religious truth for political power.[7]

The allure of such movements is strong, particularly for well-meaning Christians, but it requires deep spiritual discernment to recognize that the kingdom of God isn't defined by national borders or cultural homogeneity. The temptation to conflate religious identity with national identity is one that Christianity, when practiced authentically, must resist, for the call to follow Jesus is always a call to transcend boundaries, not to reinforce them. Christians must examine the consequences of supporting these movements as they erode unity, exacerbate polarization, and obscure the church's mission to be a global witness of reconciliation and peace.

Nick Spencer has written an excellent piece on the rise of Christian populism, where he makes many of the points I'm making in this section. Engaging with the work of Nadia Marzouki, Duncan McDonnell, and Olivier Roy, Nick Spencer writes about the problem facing Christian populism,

5. Spencer, "Rise of Christian Populism" (2017); Spencer, "Rise of Christian Populism" (2021); Roy, "Kitsch Christianity."

6. Roy, "Kitsch Christianity."

7. Coyne, "Populism and Religion"; Ryan, "Christianism."

> Christian populism pits the cause of Christian identity over and against the cause of Christian theology. The pseudo-Christian badge that stands as a cipher for my culture and nation takes precedence over its actual theological content. A Christian nation becomes a nation full of people who call themselves Christians rather than one full of people who live like Christians. Throughout, the focus is on me and others like me, rather than the "Other" . . . . Christian identity minus Christian theology allows you to speak of Christian people or Christian nation without properly scrutinizing either of those terms. It allows you to speak of Christian values without realizing how similar they are to your natural or national values. It allows you to say "no" to the other, without thinking through how you might also say "yes." Ultimately, it turns Christianity into a tool for political ends, rather than politics a tool for Christian ends.[8]

POPULISM IN THE AMERICAS: FROM THE UNITED STATES TO LATIN AMERICA

Populism has also found fertile ground in the Americas, both in the United States and across Latin America, where leaders have invoked religious language to bolster their political power. In the United States, the presidency of Donald Trump became a focal point for right-wing populism, particularly among evangelical Christians. Trump's campaign, with its slogan "Make America Great Again," tapped into a nostalgic longing for a past framed as a golden age of Christian virtue and national greatness.

I recall being in New York six months before the 2016 presidential election when some of my American friends told me there was no way Donald Trump would win. I felt compelled to disagree with them at the time, given the sentiments I saw being expressed by American evangelicals and the disenfranchisement I noticed among many working-class Americans, especially in Christian circles. People seemed fed up with the status quo, left behind by the system, distanced from social changes, and desperate for a return to "Christian values." I felt there was an excellent chance Trump could win the election by appealing to those significant feelings among large parts of the American people.

Many evangelical leaders and believers saw Trump as a kind of modern-day "Cyrus," a chosen figure tasked with restoring God's favor to the

8. Spencer, "Rise of Christian Populism" (2021); Marzouki et al., *Saving the People.*

nation. Despite Trump's personal life often conflicting with core Christian ethics, his embrace of religious rhetoric and promises to defend Christian values won the allegiance of millions.[9] The fervor with which specific segments of the church rallied behind him illustrates the seductive power of populism when it's tied to religious symbolism, even as it ignores the very heart of Christian discipleship.[10]

At the same time, Latin American populist figures such as Hugo Chávez in Venezuela and Jair Bolsonaro in Brazil have sought similar alliances with the church, utilizing religious language to support their political agendas. Chávez, though openly secular in his policies, adopted a populist style that emphasized the welfare of the "people," often appealing to the Catholic Church's social teachings to justify his socialist reforms.

Conversely, Bolsonaro in Brazil has closely aligned himself with conservative evangelical groups, presenting himself as a defender of Christian values against the secular left. For many conservative Christians in Brazil, Bolsonaro's tough-on-crime rhetoric and promises to protect "family values" resonated deeply despite his controversial and inflammatory comments. In both cases, religious language was co-opted for political power, reflecting the ways populism can be a cross-ideological phenomenon that ensnares Christians regardless of their political leanings.[11]

Yet, in these diverse contexts, populism's use of religion often represents a distortion of Christian witness. Whether from the right or left, populism's simplistic answers to complex issues (such as blaming the "other" for societal problems) tend to reduce Christianity to a tool for political manipulation. As believers, Christians are called to resist the temptation to place their hope in charismatic leaders or to elevate any political figure to messianic status.

The gospel demands a more discerning engagement with the world, one that seeks justice, mercy, and humility rather than political dominance or ideological purity. The church's role in this moment is clear: to listen to people's struggles, pains, and dreams with compassion (many common, working-class people feel silenced and ignored) while, at the same time, rejecting populism's idolatry and instead commit to the long, patient work of reconciliation and truth, even when it runs counter to the prevailing political winds. Populism's promise of "quick fixes" for society's ills is a false

9. Coyne, "Populism and Religion."

10. DeHanas, "Sacred, Supernatural, and Apocalyptic Populism."

11. Cremer, "Religion Gap."

gospel, one that ultimately undermines the church's true mission to be the body of Christ in the world.

The gospel doesn't offer simplistic answers but instead calls us to engage with the complexity of the human experience, acknowledging both the brokenness of society and the redeeming power of God's love.

POLARIZATION AND THE EROSION OF TRUTH

Populism thrives on division, and its heartbeat is driven by anger, fear, disinformation, and misinformation. These aren't merely political forces but spiritual dangers that undermine the very core of Christian life. The Christian scriptures repeatedly warn against such postures and practices, advocating instead love, compassion, trust, reconciliation, inclusion, generosity, and truth.[12]

James 3:13–18 speaks into these challenges, contrasting divisive, selfish, and demonic "wisdom" with the peace-loving, considerate, and impartial wisdom that comes from heaven.

> Who is wise and understanding among you? Let them show it by their good life, by deeds done in the humility that comes from wisdom. But if you harbor bitter envy and selfish ambition in your hearts, do not boast about it or deny the truth. Such "wisdom" does not come down from heaven but is earthly, unspiritual, demonic. For where you have envy and selfish ambition, there you find disorder and every evil practice. But the wisdom that comes from heaven is first of all pure; then peace-loving, considerate, submissive, full of mercy and good fruit, impartial and sincere. Peacemakers who sow in peace reap a harvest of righteousness.[13]

Jesus calls his followers to be bearers of truth, to speak it in love, and to uphold it in all aspects of life (Eph 4:15). The ninth commandment speaks directly to this ethical imperative: "You shall not give false testimony against your neighbor" (Exod 20:16).[14] Populism frequently betrays this command. Populist rhetoric often casts those who disagree as the enemy,

12. Scripture consistently warns against disunity and falsehood in both Testaments. E.g., Prov 6:16–19; Gal 5:19–21; Eph 4:1–6.

13. James 3:13–18 offers a robust moral vision rooted in humility and peace. For interpretive insights, see Moo, *Letter of James*.

14. Ephesians 4:15 and Exod 20:16 are often cited in Christian ethics for their emphasis on truth-telling and community integrity. Hays, *Moral Vision of the New Testament*, 61–65.

fueling narratives that distort facts, inflame passions, and dehumanize the "other." What happens when Christians are swept up in these currents? We risk losing our grounding in truth, falling prey to echo chambers that celebrate fear and division rather than compassion and reconciliation.

The challenge for Christ's disciples is profound: in an age where misinformation can spread like wildfire through social media, how do we, as the church, cultivate truth-telling and unity? Populism, whether on the left or right, thrives by exploiting our fears and turning them against our neighbors. It thrives in the spaces where we fail to practice discernment and where partisan loyalties trump the gospel's call to love our enemies. Populism doesn't just divide the nation; it fractures the church. Congregations become divided factions, as political allegiance becomes a litmus test for Christian fellowship. Families that once shared a common faith and vision are torn apart by divisive rhetoric. The question isn't just how we engage with the world but how we engage with one another within the body of Christ.

Our Lord Jesus Christ calls Christian leaders to guide their flocks through these stormy waters, to preach the truth with courage, even when it contradicts the popular narrative. This is no small task. It requires addressing the ways we're complicit in slander, gossip, misinformation, and scapegoating. It calls for teaching media discernment so that the truth isn't lost in the din of partisan noise. The church must offer an alternative to the culture of outrage and division, modeling a way that transcends the tribalism of populism.

The witness of the church must not mirror the worst aspects of the political culture but stand as a lighthouse of truth, speaking in love even when the world speaks in hate. We're called to be a people who speak the truth, but we must tell it in love, even about our political opponents. Only then will the church be the church, truly the salt and light in a world that desperately needs it.

THE CALL TO JUSTICE AND MERCY VS. SCAPEGOATING

Populist movements, by their very nature, thrive on the principle of scapegoating: blaming societal ills on a designated "enemy," often those who are already vulnerable or marginalized.[15] Whether immigrants, refugees,

15. Scapegoating theory has theological underpinnings in René Girard's work. Girard, *I See Satan Fall Like Lightning*, especially chs. 2 and 3.

religious minorities, persons addicted to substances, ethnic minorities, or those experiencing poverty, the narrative is almost always the same: "They" are the reason for the problems facing "us."

This kind of political scapegoating runs contrary to the Christian gospel, which calls for a radically different ethic. The gospel doesn't make scapegoats of others; it calls us to seek justice for the oppressed and mercy for the vulnerable. The message of Jesus, from his proclamation of the Beatitudes to his parables, consistently reverses the world's value system, lifting up the poor, the mourners, the meek, and the marginalized as the very ones who are blessed in God's kingdom. Jesus includes, honors, and welcomes those often shunned and scapegoated by society and religious institutions.[16]

The ethical challenge for the church is clear: Will we side with the gospel's call to care for the stranger and the outsider, or will we succumb to the populist temptation of casting blame and dehumanizing those who differ from us? The Bible repeatedly calls God's people to protect the weak and stand up for justice.

In Lev 19:33–34, the Israelites are commanded to love the foreigner as they love themselves: "When a foreigner resides among you in your land, do not mistreat them. The foreigner residing among you must be treated as your native-born. Love them as you would yourself, for you were once foreigners in Egypt. I am the Lord your God."[17] This isn't a call to ideological purity or national preference; it's a call to radical inclusion grounded in the love of God for all people. Love the stranger, foreigner, immigrant, vulnerable, and enemy as yourself, showing them compassion, generosity, forgiveness, honor, and kindness, just as God has done for you.

But this isn't easy. Populism offers quick, simplistic answers that blame the "other" for everything wrong in society, making it all too tempting for Christians to align with. Yet, the gospel demands more. It calls us to stand up for the dignity of the marginalized, even when doing so contradicts the loud voices of populist rhetoric. Pastors, church leaders, congregations, families, and individual disciples must speak truth to power, even when the crowd is clamoring for scapegoats. The call to mercy and justice is a prophetic stance, often demanding courage. Standing up for those who are maligned by populist movements means standing against the prevailing

16. Jesus's reversal of social values is a central theme in liberation theology. Gutiérrez, *Theology of Liberation*; also, Matt 5:1–12; Luke 14:12–14.

17. Lev 19:33–34; Brueggemann, *Theology of the Old Testament*.

winds of fear and division. It means calling the church to be the voice of compassion in a world that seeks to demonize the "other."

The church's role is to break the cycle of blame and model the way of mercy, peacemaking, and inclusion that Jesus embodied. When the church allows itself to be caught up in the populist fever of blaming and scapegoating, it loses its witness. However, when the church dares to live out the countercultural gospel, it becomes a beacon of hope and justice in a divided world. The call to love our neighbors, even those who are different, isn't an option; it's the essence of the kingdom of God, and it's the task to which Jesus Christ calls his church in these troubled times.

LISTENING TO THE WOUNDS BEHIND THE RAGE AND SHOWING EMPATHY FOR POPULISM'S DISLOCATED

At the heart of the rise of populism lies not just an ideological distortion but a spiritual failure of the church itself. We've often failed to listen deeply, to attend to the woundedness that lies beneath the rage. There is, in every community that rallies to the banner of populism, a pain that has long gone unacknowledged. It's a pain born of loss: the loss of livelihoods, the erosion of cultural identity, the collapse of once-thriving communities, the loss of meaning and purpose, and the slow death of dignity. This pain isn't just individual but collective, and it's a wound that the church has often failed to tend.

I recently listened to a podcast with Arlie Russell Hochschild about the shame and pain of working-class Americans and their attraction to populism.[18] She shared stories of coal miners in Appalachia watching their worlds crumble as the mines that once sustained their families closed their doors. Their town, once vibrant and full of life, now sits abandoned, a poignant symbol of a forgotten past. Or consider the immigrant factory worker living on the edge of survival, trapped in a cycle of exploitative wages, their dreams of a better life slowly suffocated by the weight of unrelenting poverty. These aren't isolated stories but shared narratives of loss, erasure, and being overlooked by both the systems that govern and the communities they once called home. This is the ache that populism exploits: the shame of being unseen and forgotten.

The populist movement has learned to feed on this pain. It offers a simple, if dangerous, balm: a scapegoat, a villain to blame, and a promise

18. Leonhardt and Hochschild, "It's Not Just Trump Voters."

of revenge disguised as justice. But before Christians hasten to condemn the rage of populism, we must pause and ask: What lies beneath the rage? What grief and shame are being expressed through this fiery rhetoric? We mustn't rush to label the anger as merely morally deficient; instead, we must sit with the rage long enough to hear its story, pain, suffering, shame, and desires. We must open ourselves to the painful truth that, for many, their sense of place, dignity, and worth has been chipped away over generations. As sociologist Arlie Russell Hochschild observes, for many working-class communities, there is a profound sense of estrangement, not just from the political system but from the very fabric of society itself.[19] These communities feel adrift, not just economically but culturally, morally, and spiritually. Social elites view them as backward, obsolete, and irrelevant. In this abyss, where they're dismissed, scapegoated, and disregarded, demagogues step in and offer a distorted kind of belonging, an identity built on revenge rather than reconciliation, a sense of purpose that's anchored in resentment rather than hope.

The task of the church in this context isn't to endorse populist rhetoric or lend its voice to the forces of division. It isn't to condone racism, xenophobia, or violence when they arise as expressions of this pain. But neither can the church afford to dismiss those who are hurting, those who feel forgotten. The church's task, instead, is to move into the pain with empathy, to listen not just to the words but to the wounds that lie beneath them. The church must embody a ministry of compassionate proximity. We must draw near, listen with tenderness, and honor the real grief that's often masked by anger. Jesus, in his ministry, didn't simply issue commands from a distance; he drew near to the outcast, the oppressed, and the marginalized.[20] He wept with those who mourned, he touched those who were untouchable, he sat with their pain, he empathized with their suffering, and he listened to the deep cries of those whose dignity had been trampled. Jesus's response wasn't to dismiss their pain but to enter into it. He didn't offer slogans or shallow solutions, but he met people with truth and with tears. As his disciples, we're called to model this same posture, even when the pain we encounter is expressed in the form of resentment, anger, or frustration.

19. Hochschild, *Strangers in Their Own Land.*

20. Luke 7:13; Matt 9:36; John 11:35. For reflection on Jesus's ministry of presence with the wounded, see Nouwen, *Wounded Healer.*

This listening posture isn't naive. It doesn't excuse or justify the harmful ideologies that might accompany populism: racism, xenophobia, and violence. However, it recognizes something crucial: healing doesn't begin with condemnation; it starts with empathy, with a willingness to be present in the suffering and to listen with an open heart. This is where the church can offer something the populist movement cannot: a place where people are truly seen and heard, where their stories can be told and their wounds acknowledged before God. Churches that offer spaces for honest dialogue, where people from all walks of life (whether rural, urban, immigrant, or native-born) can share their grief, pain, and lament, provide an alternative to the bitterness that populism thrives on. In these sacred spaces of shared vulnerability, the Spirit can begin to work in ways that political movements never can, mending what has been broken and restoring hope to those who have lost it.

If the church can be a place where truth and tenderness dwell together, it can become the answer to the populist cry to be remembered. For the heart of the gospel (the heart of the kingdom of God) is the message of reconciliation, of healing, of hope. It's a gospel that doesn't erase or dismiss the pain but brings healing in its fullness. Only a community that is committed to both justice and mercy can truly answer the deep cry of the disillusioned and forgotten. The call is clear: to listen with empathy, to respond with compassion, and to proclaim a gospel that brings reconciliation to a world broken by division and hate. The gospel is a balm, but it must be applied with hands that have touched the wounds of the hurting. The church is the body of Christ; Jesus calls us to bring his healing touch to the places where the world's shame and wounds are most profound. This is the mission of the gospel, and it is the mission of the church.

PRACTICING EMPATHY AND LISTENING

In a world torn apart by populism, where fear and division often prevail over understanding, Jesus calls his disciples to a different way: a way that seeks the face of God in the stranger, the outcast, the immigrant, the refugee, the foreigner, the enemy, the brother, the sister, and the "other."[21] The practice of empathy and intentional listening stands as a powerful

21. Matthew 25:35–40 and Gen 1:26–27 ground human dignity and divine image in Christian anthropology.

countermeasure against the hardening effects of populist rhetoric. It requires more than just passive tolerance; it asks for the active engagement of the heart.

The way of Jesus requires Christians to reach across dividing lines (whether cultural, political, religious, racial, gendered, or ideological) and listen to the stories of those labeled as enemies or outsiders. This might involve befriending an immigrant family or making space for the voice of a political or religious adversary. But the heart of the practice is the commitment to see the humanity of the other, to recognize in them the divine image, and to open oneself to the radical love that God commands. In this way, empathy becomes a devotional act, one that softens the heart and replaces fear with compassion.[22]

Empathy and listening are spiritual disciplines that shape our spiritual lives, helping us to imitate Jesus Christ.[23] Empathy is both a posture and a practice. When used with intentionality and consistency, it forms our spiritual lives so that we reflect the compassion, empathy, and love of Christ. You and I need to be humble and vulnerable to engage regularly with people who are different from us, acknowledging the limitations of our understandings and convictions. When we seek to live as people of empathy and attention to others, we become attuned to God's heart and purposes in the world.

As we listen deeply, we allow the Holy Spirit to transform our posture, shifting us from an "us vs. them" mentality to one of love, prayer, and active peace-building.[24] It's easy to build falls of animosity, fear, suspicion, superiority, mistrust, and division. Still, Jesus calls us to follow his example and become bridge-builders, nurturing understanding in a polarized world. As we seek conversations based on mutual respect, we break down walls, barriers, and divisions and reach across divides with love and grace.

We break free from the echo chambers of division, praying for those we once saw as enemies, and begin to embody the inclusive love of God. Do you want to manifest God's justice and mercy? Be a person of empathy and a good listener. These practices honor the dignity of others, affirm their worth as loved by God, and begin the processes required for reconciliation,

22. Nouwen, *Reaching Out.*

23. Foster, *Celebration of Discipline.*

24. Volf, *Exclusion and Embrace.*

justice, healing, and peace. Empathy is prophetic, standing against the scapegoating and demonization often propagated by populist movements.[25]

PRAYERS OF INTERCESSION FOR POLITICAL LEADERS AND OPPONENTS

In the face of populism's divisive fury, the New Testament calls us to a radically different posture: one of intercession, even for those we disagree with.[26] The practice of praying for political leaders (especially those whose actions trouble us) holds transformative power for individuals and communities. It subverts the anger, fear, and contempt that populism often stirs within us, replacing it with grace and humility.

It's difficult to demonize someone you consistently lift before God's throne, praying for their guidance, wisdom, and peace. Prayer has the power to shape our hearts so they reflect the heart of God, including God's astonishing, extravagant love. When we pray for our enemies, especially those in positions of power, it radically expands our capacity for love. We love because God loves and because God is love.[27] Intercession for those we perceive as "other" invites us into a deeper experience of God's transformative grace, softening our hearts and inviting us to see them not as enemies but as fellow image-bearers in need of God's mercy. In praying for others, we allow God to work in us, cultivating a love that transcends division.

Praying regularly for a political leader with whom you strongly disagree brings a deeper alignment to God's will, reminding you that God's grace extends beyond partisan lines. Interceding for those in power breaks the cycle of retaliation and revenge, turning our hearts toward reconciliation rather than revenge. Populist rhetoric encourages a divisive spirit of retribution, but through prayer, we actively choose to sow seeds of peace. Our prayers serve as a counter-narrative to the prevailing rhetoric of blame, inviting a more peaceful and humble posture that seeks the flourishing of all, not just the victory of one group over another.

Similarly, the communal practice of interceding for political leaders in church worship not only aligns our hearts with God's kingdom but forms us into a countercultural community. It challenges us to pray for justice: not merely the outcomes we desire, but for God's peace to reign through all

25. Girard, *I See Satan Fall Like Lightning.*

26. 1 Tim 2:1–2; Matt 5:44.

27. 1 John 4:7–8.

political systems. In this way, we engage with the Psalms of justice, praying for leaders who defend the weak and crush oppression, allowing our political perspectives to shift from partisan fervor to a deeper longing for God's righteousness.[28] This practice shapes a vision of leadership founded on mercy, service, humility, love, righteousness, and divine justice, far from the divisive politics of empire.

Praying for political leaders becomes a spiritual discipline that requires intentionality and commitment. It draws us out of our comfort zones, where it's easy to succumb to the temptation of speaking ill or harboring resentment toward those in power. Instead, prayer invites us to confront our own biases, seek God's kingdom first, and cultivate an attitude of humility. This discipline shapes our identity as citizens of a kingdom that isn't of this world, where our ultimate allegiance is to God's will, not earthly politics.[29]

MEDIA AND RHETORIC DISCERNMENT CHECKLIST

Traditional and new forms of media wield immense power, often manipulating narratives and shaping public opinion. As followers of the Jesus Way, our Lord calls us to a higher standard of discernment. Populism thrives on divisive rhetoric, so Christians must guard their hearts against content that stokes anger, fear, division, polarization, lack of empathy, disinformation, and misinformation.[30] The question isn't only whether the content is accurate but also whether it nurtures the love of God and one's neighbor.

We must ask: Does this content make us more compassionate, kind, holy, and just, or does it lead to darker places that contradict the gospel, way, and Spirit of Jesus Christ? Does this source encourage me to see others with compassion, or does it fuel contempt and division? Is it grounded in truth, or does it thrive on unverified rumors and sensationalism? The wisdom of Phil 4:8, to think about what is true, honorable, and commendable, offers a profound guide in navigating this space. If I were to paraphrase Paul's advice, I'd do so this way: "Finally, followers of the Jesus Way, ambassadors of God's kingdom, disciples who serve the God of truth, reconciliation, and love: whatever is true, whatever is noble, whatever is right, whatever is pure, whatever is lovely, whatever is admirable (if anything is excellent or

28. Ps 72:1–4; Ps 82:1–4.

29. John 18:36; cf. O'Donovan, *Desire of the Nations*.

30. Norris and Inglehart, *Cultural Backlash*.

praiseworthy) think about such things." Imagine how our consumption of online, new, and traditional media would change if we filtered it through that lens.

It's tempting to chase after viral news cycles, trending stories, or politically motivated narratives, especially when these feed bandwagons, arouse an audience, or help us establish our reputation or brand. But God calls Christians to dedicate themselves to truth, not popularity, and to be seekers of the light, not noise.[31] Sometimes, the truth is inconvenient, goes against the grain of prevailing opinions, or contradicts our long-held assumptions and biases. Regardless, our God requires us to pause and reflect, seeking the truth rather than aligning ourselves with the loudest voices. Pursuing truth is foundational to our media engagement, helping us act as people of honesty, courage, integrity, and the gospel of Jesus Christ.

The "three-day rule" (waiting three days before reacting to a sensational story) can help Christians pause and allow the truth to emerge, ensuring that their response isn't hasty or influenced by populist propaganda. Seeking out voices from Christians of differing political perspectives can also serve as a humbling practice.

We also need a media diet that reflects the values of God's kingdom (not avoiding other forms of media, which can help us appreciate what's going on in the world, but spending the bulk of our time intentionally consuming sources that promote values of peace, reconciliation, and unity, rather than fueling further division). This includes seeking out media that uplifts marginalized voices, promotes the well-being of the oppressed, and challenges systems of injustice.[32] Such a media diet helps us grow spiritually and also supports voices that advocate for empathy, truth, reconciliation, unity, and love.

These discerning approaches to traditional and new media nurture a spirit of peacemaking, making us not merely consumers of media but active truth-tellers who refuse to be manipulated by fear-driven narratives.

THE FRUIT TEST (GALATIANS 5)

The "fruit test," drawn from Gal 5:19–23, provides a vital spiritual barometer for Christians seeking to discern the integrity of political movements or leaders. Paul's words contrast the acts of the flesh (hatred, discord, rage, and

31. Ellul, *Humiliation of the Word*.

32. Gutiérrez, *Theology of Liberation*.

dissension) with the fruit of the Spirit, which are love, joy, peace, patience, kindness, goodness, faithfulness, gentleness, and self-control.

This profound yet straightforward test helps believers measure the spiritual health of the causes they support. When a movement or leader consistently breeds division, anger, or fear, it's a clear signal that it's out of alignment with God's kingdom. Conversely, when a cause promotes kindness, humility, and peace, we can be confident that God's Spirit is at work.

The fruit test teaches us that the ends don't justify the means; even a righteous cause can be tainted if it resorts to deceit, hatred, or violence.[33] Pastors, parents, and others can guide their congregations, families, colleagues, neighbors, and friends to monitor their hearts, ensuring that they aren't drawn into unhealthy anger, mistrust, scapegoating, or fervor.

If a political engagement makes us feel more anxious or angry, it's time to step back and reassess our approach. The fruit test calls us to recalibrate our actions and attitudes so that they align with the love and justice of God, counteracting the divisive and manipulative forces of populism.

The fruit of the Spirit holds up a mirror to our character and Christlikeness. How we respond to external events and the provocations and rhetoric of political leaders and movements can reveal the condition of our hearts. Are we a people of love, kindness, self-control, and peace, or are our hearts consumed by (or swept up in) division and anger? The "fruit test" invites us to examine our hearts, values, interactions, and reactions in light of the values of the kingdom of God and the qualities of the Spirit of Jesus Christ. We can pause and ask: "Am I exhibiting the love, joy, and peace that Christ calls me to, even amid political fervor?"

The world is watching. Are we truly following Jesus and embodying his Way? Are we swept up in ideological and political battles that eclipse moral and spiritual clarity? Are we resisting the temptation to fall into the traps of anger and fear that populist movements and leaders often fuel, and instead, living as people of grace, love, peace, and reconciliation? When loud voices call for division or retribution, are we people of hope and reconciliation who, instead, proclaim the fruit of the Spirit: kindness, goodness, and gentleness? How we respond to politics, conflicts, divisions, and leadership speaks volumes to the world about the transforming power of Jesus Christ. The fruit test helps enable us to be ambassadors of God's kingdom, showing

33. Hauerwas, *Peaceable Kingdom*; Bonhoeffer, *Ethics*.

the world that true power isn't in force, might, or political opinions but in vulnerability, love, humility, and the way of the cross of Christ.[34]

POPULISM AND CHRISTIAN NATIONALISM ACROSS THE US POLITICAL SPECTRUM

Before turning to the historical failures of the church under empire and what we can learn from them, let's briefly examine how populist and Christian nationalist rhetoric has emerged across the United States political spectrum (right and left) over recent decades.

Populism has long shaped American political discourse, surfacing in both Republican and Democratic rhetoric. At its core, populism frames politics as a battle between "the pure people" and "the corrupt elite," often bypassing institutions in favor of direct appeals to the public's will.[35] However, not all populist rhetoric constitutes ideological populism, and not all populism is paired with Christian nationalism.

On the political right, Donald Trump exemplifies classic right-wing populism. His slogans (e.g., "I am your voice" and "drain the swamp") cast Washington insiders, the media, and global institutions as enemies of ordinary Americans.[36] Trump also embraced Christian nationalism, promoting the idea that America has a divinely ordained mission. His support base included groups that merged Christian identity with national destiny, seen starkly during the January 6 Capitol riot, where Christian flags and prayers accompanied political violence.

Sarah Palin also fused right-wing populism with Christian nationalist sentiment, frequently describing the United States as a Christian nation and casting herself as a God-fearing outsider confronting the secular elite.[37] Ronald Reagan, while invoking biblical imagery like the "city on a hill," leaned more toward civil religion than overt Christian nationalism.[38] His rhetoric emphasized moral renewal and small government rather than a theocratic national identity.

On the left, figures like Bernie Sanders and Elizabeth Warren have employed populist rhetoric but avoided Christian nationalism entirely.

34. Wright, *Day the Revolution Began.*
35. Mudde and Kaltwasser, *Populism.*
36. Trump, "Nomination Acceptance Speech."
37. Palin, "Speech at the Republican National Convention."
38. Reagan, "Vision for America."

Sanders, with slogans like "the billionaire class can't have it all," identifies corporate elites as the main threat to the people and calls for democratic socialism grounded in economic justice.[39] He champions pluralism and is strongly secular. Warren's language (e.g., "the system is rigged") reflects populist tones, though her approach is more technocratic and reformist than revolutionary.[40]

Historically, Huey Long embodied left-wing populism, advocating for radical wealth redistribution under the banner "Every man a king."[41] Yet religion played little role in his agenda, and he remained detached from Christian nationalist themes.

While populism is evident across the political spectrum, Christian nationalism is primarily associated with right-wing populist movements in the United States. It combines nationalism with religious identity, often at the expense of pluralism and democratic norms. Left-wing populists, in contrast, tend to direct their critique toward economic elites and maintain a clear separation between faith and state power.

I offer a gentle selah as I draw these contemplations to a close: May Jesus Christ grant us the grace to pause and reflect, allowing the Spirit to guide us toward a deeper alignment with God's kingdom, where peace, truth, and love reign supreme.

39. Nicols, "Bernie Sanders."

40. Chaggaris, "Elizabeth Warren."

41. Long, *Every Man a King*, 136.

4.

The Cross in Hitler's Shadow

WHEN THE SOUL OF a nation is gripped by fear and clothed in idolatry, those of us who are followers of Jesus Christ must decide whom we truly serve. In the shadow of tyranny, it's not silence that saves us but confession that's costly, clear, and rooted in the unshakable lordship of Christ: confessing our allegiance to Jesus Christ as our sole Lord and rejecting any attempts to subordinate the church to political ideologies.

THE LORDSHIP OF CHRIST VS. THE FÜHRER PRINCIPLE

In Nazi Germany, the rise of Adolf Hitler and the perversion of power under the Führerprinzip (the Leader Principle) sought to establish the state and its leader as the ultimate authority in all aspects of life, including the church.[1] In this atmosphere, the church faced a dangerous temptation: to subordinate its allegiance to Christ and align itself with a national ideology that deified the Führer. This temptation included the possibility of aligning itself with the state to receive safety, status, legitimacy, and control. Yet, such state "gifts" would come at the cost of fidelity to the gospel of Jesus Christ and betrayal of the values of the kingdom of God.

The call of the Confessing Church, exemplified in the 1934 Barmen Declaration, was a bold theological stand for the exclusive lordship of Christ. As articulated in the Barmen Declaration: "Jesus Christ, as he is attested for us in Holy Scripture, is the one Word of God whom we have

1. Evans, *Third Reich in Power*, 15–20.

to trust and obey in life and in death."[2] This powerful assertion served as a defiant rejection of any authority that would dare to supplant the word of God, whether that authority came in the form of Hitler, the Nazi regime, or any other political movement. This declaration of the supreme lordship and sovereignty of Jesus Christ was a radical, courageous, risky, and costly stand against the idolization of ideologies and power and a fierce statement that no political leader, ideology, or national agenda can replace Christ as Lord.

The Confessing Church's stance against the Führerprinzip wasn't an abstract theological debate; it was a matter of life and death. They understood that the ultimate allegiance of a Christian could never be compromised, even in the face of violent repression. Theologically, the church reasserted that Christ alone is the King and Head of the church, and that no other power, no matter how charismatic or powerful, could claim the same devotion. This meant rejecting the pseudo-Christian "German Christian" movement that tried to bind the church's message to nationalistic fervor, promoting the idolization of the state as an extension of Christ's rule.[3]

For the Confessing Church, the cost of discipleship wasn't merely intellectual but existential. They knew that by upholding Christ's sole authority, they were setting themselves against the very powers that controlled their survival. Yet, this allegiance, this "cost of discipleship," was understood as the only way to remain faithful to the gospel and to resist the forces of evil that sought to manipulate the church.[4]

The resistance of the Confessing Church offers a poignant example of spiritual resistance firmly grounded in the historic and immutable truths of the Christian faith. In this context, clinging to Christ's lordship wasn't mere theological abstraction but a life-or-death decision, where obedience to the word of God demanded courage, conviction, and, in many cases, personal sacrifice and even death.

THE CHURCH AS A COMMUNITY UNDER GOD'S WORD, NOT RACE OR NATION

Under Nazi rule, the church in Germany was confronted with an insidious ideology that sought to redefine the church's identity, not in Christ, but in terms of race and nation. The Nazi state promoted ideas of racial purity and

2. *Barmen Theological Declaration*, Thesis 1, 388.

3. Bergen, *Twisted Cross*.

4. Bonhoeffer, *Discipleship*, xxv–xxx.

the supremacy of the "Volk" (the people), hoping to align Christian theology with nationalistic and exclusionary ideas.

In response, the Confessing Church resisted this theological corruption, insisting that the church's identity was defined solely by faith in Christ and baptism, not by ethnicity or nationality. As the Barmen Declaration powerfully states, "The Church is solely Christ's property . . . living by His comfort and direction."[5] This declaration was an unequivocal rejection of the notion that the church could be co-opted to serve nationalistic or ideological purposes. It was a reminder that the church isn't an institution of the state but the body of Christ united in faith and bound together by the love of the Savior.

Dietrich Bonhoeffer, a pivotal figure within the Confessing Church, argued fiercely against any attempt to subordinate the church to the will of the state. In his seminal work *Discipleship*, Bonhoeffer wrote that true allegiance to Christ required the church to stand as Christ's visible body, even if that meant standing in opposition to the pressures of national identity.[6]

Bonhoeffer's radical call to discipleship, which he termed the "cost of discipleship," meant that the church would face hardship, persecution, and even death for its refusal to bow to any idol: be it the state or race. Bonhoeffer's prophetic voice stands clear in his words: "The church has only one altar, the altar of the Almighty . . . before which all creatures must kneel. Whoever seeks something other than this must keep away; he can't join us in the house of God."[7]

This declaration encapsulated the truth that no Christian altar could bear the cross of Christ and the swastika together. The church couldn't sanctify national agendas or make room for anything that sought to replace Christ with the idols of the nation-state. The church's ultimate allegiance lies with Christ alone, whose word and kingdom transcend every earthly power and whose gospel calls us to embrace the outsider, challenge unjust systems, and bear witness to the unity of all people in Christ.[8]

In this period of spiritual and cultural warfare, the Confessing Church's commitment to Christ alone wasn't only a theological stance but a radical witness of what it means to live under God's word rather than the sway of national ideologies or political pressures. As Bonhoeffer would remind us,

5. *Barmen Theological Declaration*, Thesis 4, 389.

6. Bonhoeffer, *Discipleship*, 227–35.

7. Bonhoeffer, *Cost of Discipleship*, 233.

8. Barnett, *For the Soul of the People*.

the church can't be co-opted by nationalism; it must stand firm in its call to follow Christ, no matter the cost.

THE "GERMAN CHRISTIAN" MOVEMENT VS. THE CONFESSING CHURCH

In Nazi Germany, two distinct responses to the rise of Adolf Hitler emerged within Protestantism, illustrating the tension between compromised faith and courageous resistance. The "German Christian" movement, which gained significant traction among church leaders and officials, sought to align Christianity with Hitler's nationalist and racist agenda.[9] These pro-Nazi Christians espoused the Führerprinzip (leader principle), which placed Hitler at the center of national life and framed him as the savior of Germany. They went so far as to purge the church of any elements deemed "too Jewish," even rewriting scripture to suit Nazi ideology.[10] The Old Testament was discarded, and Jesus was re-imagined as an Aryan hero who endorsed the racial superiority of the German people.

Churches, once sanctuaries of grace, were co-opted to fly the swastika, and Hitler's rule was celebrated as a divine mandate. The union of Christianity and nationalism became taken for granted by many, as the masses saw no contradiction between patriotic loyalty and Christian duty.

Against this disturbing backdrop, the Confessing Church emerged as a courageous and defiant force. In 1934, at the Barmen Synod, a group of pastors and laypeople declared their unwavering allegiance to the lordship of Christ, denouncing any attempt to subordinate the church to Nazi ideology. The Barmen Declaration, written by Karl Barth and others, proclaimed the lordship of Jesus Christ alone: "Jesus Christ, as testified to us in Holy Scripture, is the one Word of God, that we must hear, trust, and obey in life and death."[11] For the Confessing Church, Jesus Christ alone was the head of the church, and no political leader or ideology could usurp his authority.

What are the key assertions of the Barmen Declaration? Let me summarize them:

1. Exclusive Lordship of Christ: Jesus Christ, as the one Word of God revealed in holy Scripture, is the sole object of trust and obedience for

9. Bergen, *Twisted Cross.*

10. Bergen, *Twisted Cross*; Heschel, *Aryan Jesus.*

11. Busch, *Barmen Theses Then and Now*; *Barmen Theological Declaration*, 388–90.

the church. No other authority, be it political or ideological, can supplant or add to his word. This foundational belief rejects the notion that any leader, ideology, or political system can hold equal power to that of Christ over the life of the church.

2. Rejection of Ideological Syncretism: The church can't adopt any false teaching that seeks to incorporate other sources of revelation, such as the Führerprinzip (the principle of the Führer as the ultimate authority), into its theological framework. The message and order of the church must remain faithful to the gospel of Christ and shouldn't be shaped by current political convictions or ideological movements.
3. Church's Exclusive Allegiance to Christ: The church isn't to be co-opted for political or national purposes. It belongs entirely to Christ, and its mission and actions must align solely with his will. The church is called to act as a community of believers living by Christ's comfort and instruction, proclaiming the gospel in all circumstances without yielding to political pressure.
4. Rejection of State Control over the Church: The church can't allow the state to dictate its message, structure, or mission. While the state has its divinely ordained role in maintaining peace and justice, the church must maintain its autonomy, witnessing to the truth of Christ without being co-opted by political or nationalistic agendas.
5. The Church's Mission and Freedom: The church's freedom is rooted in its commission to proclaim God's grace through the Christian scriptures and sacraments. The church's role is to be a faithful witness to Christ, not a tool for fulfilling political or national objectives. The church is called to stand in the world with the freedom to preach the gospel, trusting that God's word isn't bound by human authority.

This theological stand wasn't an abstract debate but a matter of life and death. Pastors like Martin Niemöller, who was imprisoned for his opposition to Hitler, and theologians like Dietrich Bonhoeffer, who continued to resist despite mounting persecution, exemplified the cost of such witness.[12] Bonhoeffer's secret seminary at Finkenwalde was a radical attempt to preserve faithful Christian ministry free from Nazi influence.[13]

12. Barnett, *For the Soul of the People.*

13. Bonhoeffer, *Life Together*, 7–25.

These acts of resistance, at significant personal and collective cost, remain powerful reminders of the importance of standing firm in Christ's truth, even when the surrounding culture falls prey to dangerous ideologies. Their resistance, though often marginalized and persecuted, serves as a profound model for today's church in the face of political idolatries.

The Barmen Declaration raises critical questions for me and you as disciples today: How often do I allow political ideologies to influence or even redefine my message and mission? Am I faithfully proclaiming the exclusive lordship of Christ, or have I allowed other authorities (whether political, cultural, or nationalistic) to shape my convictions? In what ways do I let the state or the dominant culture influence my theological commitments, and where do I draw the line in maintaining the integrity of the gospel? Do I, like the Confessing Church, have the courage to resist ideologies that distort the truth of Christ, even when it comes at significant personal or communal cost? How does my church community reflect the lordship of Christ in its practices, leadership, and interactions with society? Do I allow myself to be swept up by populist rhetoric or nationalism, or am I committed to a faith that transcends earthly divisions and allegiances? How can I ensure that my actions and beliefs consistently align with the values of God's kingdom rather than falling prey to the temptation of idolatry or the pursuit of power? What does it mean for me, in this moment, to remain faithful to Christ's call, even when it places me in opposition to prevailing cultural or political powers?

INDIVIDUAL DISCIPLESHIP IN NAZI GERMANY AND THE COST OF OBEDIENCE

While the Confessing Church represented a collective witness to Christ's lordship over all powers, individual Christians in Nazi Germany also faced the personal cost of discipleship, standing in opposition to the empire's demands. One striking example is Franz Jägerstätter, an Austrian Catholic farmer who, in 1943, refused to swear an oath of loyalty to Hitler or serve in the Nazi military.[14] His refusal to bow to the pressure of state-sponsored ideology, despite the consequences, embodied a profound spiritual resistance. Jägerstätter believed that any allegiance to the Nazi regime would betray his loyalty to Christ.

14. Zahn, *In Solitary Witness.*

Despite the personal costs, including his execution in 1943, Jägerstätter's witness of moral courage has been recognized by the Catholic Church, which later beatified him.[15] His steadfastness in the face of immense pressure offers a stark reminder of the personal responsibility each believer has to discern God's will and resist the temptation to compromise one's faith for political expediency.

Similarly, the story of Sophie Scholl and the White Rose group of Christian university students in Munich stands as another example of individual discipleship in the face of a totalitarian regime.[16] They courageously distributed leaflets denouncing the atrocities of the Nazi regime, calling their fellow citizens to awaken to the truth of God's justice. For their efforts, Sophie Scholl and her companions were arrested and executed, yet their unwavering stance against evil has left an indelible mark on the Christian conscience. Their legacy of moral courage continues to challenge the church today, prompting believers to consider whether they will quietly conform to prevailing powers or stand for truth, justice, and love.

In a similar vein, Pastor André Trocmé in Le Chambon, France, led a community of Huguenots who sheltered Jewish refugees during the Nazi occupation, risking their own lives to protect the vulnerable.[17] Trocmé's actions embodied the "Higher Law" of God's love, which superseded the orders of the Vichy government.

These individual acts of resistance, whether through refusing to give the Nazi salute or providing sanctuary to the oppressed, illustrate the high cost of following Christ's command to love one's neighbor, even when doing so brings us into direct conflict with the powers of the world. Through these stories, we see that discipleship isn't a passive assent to religious ideas but an active, often costly commitment to live according to God's will, standing against the powers of empire, and living out a faith that challenges the status quo.

THE SLIPPERY SLOPE OF CHURCH COMPLICITY IN INJUSTICE

The history of the German church under Nazism serves as a chilling reminder of how the church can be gradually co-opted into supporting

15. Gumbleton, "Homily at the Beatification of Franz Jägerstätter."
16. Scholl, *White Rose.*
17. Hallie, *Lest Innocent Blood Be Shed.*

injustice. As we reflect on the ethical and pastoral implications of this, we must ask uncomfortable but necessary questions: How did so many baptized Christians in Nazi Germany come to endorse or acquiesce to such atrocities?

The gradual acceptance of state ideology, dressed in the garb of nationalism and racial purity, wasn't immediate. It took root when the church ceased to measure the state's actions against God's standards and began to baptize state ideologies as if they aligned with Christ's kingdom. The church's complicity didn't happen overnight; it was a slow erosion of the truth, influenced by fear, economic hardship, ethical compromise, theological shallowness, drift from the way of Jesus Christ, and the promises of political security.[18]

When we examine this in our context, the implications are clear. The church's ethical duty is to continually check its alignment with God's values, never allowing loyalty to the state to override loyalty to Christ. This means that, as followers of Jesus, we must reject any notion of "national destiny" or the idea that any ethnic group has divine supremacy. Just as Nazi propaganda exploited fear and division to justify hatred and dehumanization, we must be vigilant today. The church mustn't condone or excuse hatred, injustice, or oppression under any guise, be it political, racial, cultural, national, religious, or ideological. If we do, we risk repeating the same mistakes. The lesson from the past is stark: when the church allows politics to dictate its theology, it becomes complicit in evil.[19]

Biblical and theological education plays a critical role in forming a courageous, faithful, confessing church. The ideas that seeped into the "German Christians" demonstrate the importance of sound theological and biblical education, which teaches Christians to resist the seductive forces of power, nationalism, division, and hatred.

As Christ's disciples, we must examine ourselves, invite the Spirit to lead us toward repentance and have the courage to confront any complicity we've indulged in, both past and present. Church leaders can teach their congregations to stand against injustice and abusive uses of power, scrutinize ideologies and political claims, and nurture empathy for marginalized and vulnerable people. The history of the church's complicity in Nazi Germany challenges us: Are we willing to make that stand now before it's too late?

18. Ericksen, *Complicity in the Holocaust.*

19. Bonhoeffer, *Ethics*, 50–65.

Church leaders must remind their flocks that no regime, no matter how alluring or seemingly righteous, should ever replace Christ as the ultimate authority. The Spirit and Bible call us to cultivate hearts that refuse to be swayed by political expediency and to teach our people that the truth of God transcends national or political ideologies. Our responsibility is to help our communities recognize when propaganda and false narratives creep in and to equip them with the discernment to stand firm in God's truth.

COURAGE AND CONFESSION IN THE FACE OF CULTURAL CHRISTIANITY

Another profound implication arising from the German church's experience under Nazism is the need for the church to confess the truth, even in the face of overwhelming cultural pressure. The Confessing Church stands as a lighthouse of courage, where Christians boldly spoke the truth about God and humanity, even when it cost them dearly.[20] This truth wasn't only theological but also deeply ethical: affirming the Jewishness of Jesus, the unity of all people in Christ, and the church's independence from the state. These were dangerous truths to proclaim in Nazi Germany, where anti-Semitism and state-sponsored persecution of minorities were the official narrative.

Similarly, in today's world, Christ calls his disciples to confess truths that challenge the culture around them, whether it's affirming the equal dignity of all ethnicities in the face of rising white supremacy or standing firm in Christ's command to love immigrants and refugees in times of xenophobia.

Pastorally, this calls for the preparation of believers to be confessors, people who are willing to stand for truth in their everyday lives, regardless of the cost. This doesn't mean martyrdom for most of us, but it does mean a willingness to stand against the current when the culture around us is moving in the wrong direction.

Just as Dietrich Bonhoeffer called the church to resist the idolatry of the Nazi regime, Jesus Christ calls us to resist the idols of our time, be they nationalism, consumerism, expressive individualism, populism, or

20. Bethge, *Dietrich Bonhoeffer*.

injustice.[21] The church must be a prophetic voice for the voiceless, standing for the oppressed and marginalized, even when it's unpopular.

Today's church must take proactive steps to prepare its people for this kind of faithfulness. Let's get creative and shape spaces for wild, untamed, prophetic forms of discipleship that challenge personality cults, cultural lies, and deceptive political ideologies. Let's go deep and nurture a robust understanding of biblical, theological, and ethical truths. We can do this through study groups, accountability partnerships, and preaching that consistently calls the church back to its prophetic role. The time to make this decision is now before the prevailing winds of culture sweep us away.

Just as the Confessing Church made its stand against the Nazis, the Holy Spirit calls us to make our stand now, on the side of Christ's commands, no matter what. The faithfulness of a few can change the course of history, just as it did in Germany. May we be courageous in the face of the idols of our time and faithful to the confession that Christ is Lord.

CORPORATE CONFESSION AND LAMENT

One of the most vital practices the church must reclaim in the modern world is corporate confession and lament. History teaches us that the body of Christ, in all its beauty and brokenness, is vulnerable to complicity with injustice, even to the point of aiding and abetting evil. When we look at the tragic history of the German church under Nazism, we're confronted with the painful reality of how easily Christians can be seduced by political powers, allowing the gospel to be twisted to fit agendas of nationalism and hate.[22] The church's complicity in the suffering of others isn't a matter of distant history but an ongoing temptation we must continually resist. Corporate confession is a call to break our collective pride to acknowledge the ways we have allowed fear, comfort, or convenience to silence the prophetic voice of the gospel.

Churches today can learn from the Germans who, in the aftermath of World War II, confessed their complicity through the Stuttgart Declaration of Guilt.[23] Similarly, congregations today must take time to confess, especially during poignant seasons like Reformation Sunday, when we reflect on past failures and shortcomings. A prayerful litany of confession

21. Bonhoeffer, *Discipleship.*

22. Bergen, *Twisted Cross.*

23. "Stuttgarter Schuldbekenntnis," 438–39.

might be prayed: "Forgive us, Lord, for the times when, like our forebears in Germany, we remained silent in the face of evil. Forgive any ways we have harbored prejudice or pursued power over integrity. Have mercy and cleanse your church."

The act of corporate lamenting is also a crucial practice for healing. When the church acknowledges its role in the harm caused to marginalized groups, such as remembering the suffering of Holocaust victims, we fulfill the biblical mandate to "weep with those who weep" (Rom 12:15). This communal act of repentance keeps alive the memory of past wrongs, teaching us that complacency and silence are never neutral but serve to perpetuate injustice. By mourning together, we cultivate a collective resolve to seek justice in the present, ensuring we do not repeat the sins of the past.

On my author website, I've designed a guide for writing a lament.[24]

Here's an example of a lament, which I've written in light of the themes covered in this book:

A Lament for a Church Captive to Empire

O God of liberation and love,

We cry out to you from the ruins of a compromised witness.

You are the God who sets captives free,

Who leads people not into domination but into communion.

Yet we confess: your church has bowed before the empires of this world.

We have mistaken nationalism for discipleship and conquest for calling.

Your name has been invoked to justify violence, racism, politics, and colonization.

We have wrapped the cross in flags and forgotten the cost of love.

O Christ, crucified and risen,

You did not ride the war horse of Caesar but entered on a donkey.

You are a servant King, a wounded Healer,

Yet, we have forged you into the image of our power and pride.

We lament how your church has silenced prophets and canonized tyrants,

24. Hill, "How to Write a Lament."

Crucified peacemakers and crowned emperors.

Forgive us, O God,

For the times we loved influence more than integrity,

And the myth of empire more than the message of the kingdom.

We have turned your gospel of grace into a weapon,

And preached exclusion where you extended welcome.

We grieve the churches built on stolen land,

The theologies used to enslave, the prayers said in conquest.

We confess: our idols are many.

Comfort. Nation. Race. Control. Certainty.

Break our hardened hearts,

And teach us again to follow the way of the cross.

Raise up among us a new imagination,

Not of domination but of service and sacrifice.

Give us the courage to confront false gospels,

And to repent where we've been complicit in harm.

Rekindle in us the dream of your reign,

Where swords are beaten into plowshares and enemies into kin.

You are our hope and refuge,

We cry out to you when all seems lost and when powers threaten.

May your Spirit dismantle what empire has built and fear has constructed,

And breathe new life into communities of justice, humility, love, and peace.

Lead us to the margins,

Where you already dwell among the broken and cast aside.

Remind us that borders do not protect the kingdom of God,

But revealed in bread shared, feet washed, hearts reconciled, and tables expanded.

We lament the past, but we do not lose hope.

You are the God who brings resurrection out of crucifixion.

Restore your church, O Christ,

Not to power but to faithfulness.

May our lips proclaim that there is only one King,

Our Lord and Savior, Jesus Christ.

Fill us with passion for the shalom, reconciliation, and liberation of your kingdom,

Not the violence, division, and bondage of earthly empires.

May we bear witness to your reign,

On earth as it is in heaven.

Through Jesus Christ our Lord,

Amen.

STUDYING AND PRAYING THE BARMEN DECLARATION AND SIMILAR CONFESSIONS

In times of moral and ideological crisis, Christians need to turn to the words of faithful believers who have gone before us, and the Barmen Declaration stands as a powerful resource for the church today. The six theses crafted in 1934 by the Confessing Church provide a robust theological framework that continues to speak prophetically to us.[25] Each of these theses offers profound wisdom on how to resist the temptation to align the gospel with the prevailing powers of our time.

The first thesis, for instance, boldly declares, "Jesus Christ . . . is the one Word of God whom we must hear and obey in life and death."[26] This simple but profound statement invites us to examine our hearts and lives. What "words" or ideologies are we currently listening to? What voices are we giving authority in our lives? In times when cultural and political winds threaten to sway our allegiance, the Barmen Declaration reminds us that there is only one Word of God that demands our trust and obedience: Jesus Christ.

Believers can incorporate these theses into personal and communal spiritual practices. A small group or individual might choose to reflect on

25. Busch, *Barmen Theses Then and Now*.

26. *Barmen Theological Declaration*, Thesis 1, 388.

how each thesis applies to the modern world, asking questions like, "What are the modern-day 'earthly powers' that present themselves as sources of revelation or ultimate authority?" This reflective exercise brings clarity, especially in the face of ideological and political pressure to compromise.

A powerful spiritual practice would be to memorize a line from Barmen, such as, "We reject the false doctrine that the Church can surrender the form of its message to suit the wishes of the current ideological and political convictions," and recall this line when tempted to dilute the gospel to fit cultural trends.[27] For those in traditions with a Reformation heritage, such as those inspired by the Barmen Declaration, using confessions like the Belhar Confession from South Africa or other historic declarations as devotional materials can serve as a powerful means to deepen one's spiritual life.[28]

These confessions shouldn't be relegated to the past as museum pieces but treated as living documents that can fortify and challenge us today. In praying through these confessions, we join with a great cloud of witnesses, those who resisted evil with faith, and stand in continuity with those who refused to bow to false ideologies. This continuity emboldens us to stand firm in the face of pressure, knowing that the gospel is always countercultural and demands our allegiance to Christ alone.

"RED-FLAG" INDICATORS OF CHURCH COMPROMISE

The church must always be vigilant, especially when threatened with the subtle entanglements of politics and power. The history of the German church under Nazi rule serves as a blunt caution about how compromise can sneak in undetected, eroding the church's witness and integrity.

One of the key indicators that a church is compromising with an unhealthy ideology is the gradual insertion of national or racial symbols into worship spaces. The church's chief symbol (the cross) can be easily eclipsed when symbols like swastikas or nationalist imagery are given equal prominence. In Nazi Germany, the church halls embellished with Hitler portraits and the swastika in the place of the crucifix were a sharp sign that the gospel was no longer the principal message.[29] Today, similar signs

27. *Barmen Theological Declaration*, Thesis 3, 389.

28. Boesak and DeYoung, *Radical Reconciliation*, 87–95; *Belhar Confession* (online).

29. Bergen, *Twisted Cross*.

can be observed when nationalism permeates the church's messages and liturgies, calling Christians to allegiance to a nation over loyalty to Christ.

Another marker of compromise is the backing of political leaders as quasi-divine figures. When clergy begin to elevate and promote leaders, suggesting they are divinely chosen or immune from scrutiny, it's a potent red flag. If political rhetoric starts to take precedence over the preaching of Scripture, it's another indication that a political agenda is co-opting the church. The German church saw this happen with the "German Christians" movement, which distorted and deformed Christian doctrine to fit Nazi ideology, even stripping Christianity of its Jewish roots.[30]

These early compromises, such as the exclusion of Jewish Christians under pressure, set the stage for even more disastrous ones. This "red-flag" tool encourages believers to ask themselves tough questions when they sense something is off.

When church practices or messages seem more aligned with party platforms and cultural myths than with the word of God, it's time to take a step back. We must ask tough questions. Are we still being led by Jesus Christ, the Bible, and the Holy Spirit, or are we being shaped by the powerful forces around us? Have we compromised with the ideologies and political agendas of our age, or are we maintaining a faithful, prophetic, loving witness to Jesus Christ and his gospel and kingdom?

Vigilance is the key. We can't afford not to be watchful. Compromise is insidious and gradual; faithfulness and vigilance are demanding and easily relinquished. We need spaces for ethical discernment and honest conversations. Our commitment must be to safeguard ourselves against the gradual erosion of truth. The goal is to act early before compromise sets in, keeping the church's witness pure and unyielding to earthly powers.

INTERPRETING ROMANS 13 AND 1 PETER 2 IN CONTEXT

One of the most dangerous misapplications of Scripture in Nazi Germany was the interpretation of passages like Rom 13:1, which urges Christians to "be subject to the governing authorities."[31] This verse, often quoted by the "German Christians" movement, was used to justify unconditional obedience to Hitler's regime, even as it perpetrated grave injustices. However, the

30. Heschel, *Aryan Jesus.*

31. De Gruchy, *Bonhoeffer and South Africa.*

interpretation of this verse (and others like it in 1 Pet 2) requires careful attention to the broader context of Scripture. Paul and Peter did indeed affirm respect for rulers, but they didn't teach blind obedience to evil. The same apostle who wrote, "Honor the emperor" also boldly declared before the Sanhedrin, "We must obey God rather than people" (Acts 5:29).[32]

Romans 13:1–4 and 1 Pet 2:13–14 have been wielded as weapons and offered as guidance. They speak of submission to governing authorities, of rulers as agents of order. But to read them flatly, without context, is to miss their ache and depth. Paul and Peter wrote these words under an empire that was flawed, violent, and imperial. And still, they dared to imagine a deeper allegiance.

Submission here isn't blind obedience. It's not baptizing tyranny or sacralizing injustice. It's a call to live peaceably, discerning the good, resisting evil, and embodying a cross-shaped witness. When authorities protect the vulnerable and pursue what's right, we honor that work. When they devour the weak or idolize power, our call is prophetic, not partisan.

This discipleship isn't quietism. It's courageous humility. To submit isn't to cower but to live so faithfully that our lives shine a light on what governments should be: just, accountable, and servants of the common good. Peter and Paul both died by state violence. Yet neither became violent themselves.

These verses aren't a shield for empire. They're a summons to live as those whose ultimate authority is Christ: crucified, risen, reigning. And in that allegiance, we hold power accountable, honor peace, and walk the long road of suffering love.

Submission to authority isn't absolute; it's contingent on the authority remaining within God's moral boundaries. God's ultimate authority can't be subjugated to any earthly ruler who acts outside of righteousness. This distinction is crucial. Scripture provides numerous examples of godly resistance to corrupt authority, from Daniel's defiance of King Nebuchadnezzar's idol-worship decree to the Hebrew midwives' refusal to comply with Pharaoh's genocidal orders.[33] Each of these acts of resistance is commended in Scripture, making it clear that submission is not the same as passive compliance when authorities act in direct contradiction to God's will.

This approach to understanding passages such as Rom 13 and 1 Pet 2 offers a vital safeguard against the misuse of Scripture by authoritarian

32. Acts 5:29; Rom 13:1; 1 Pet 2:13–14.

33. Exod 1:15–21; Dan 3:13–18.

figures. In today's world, when governments or leaders pass laws that contradict the teachings of Christ, Christians must have the courage to dissent.

A helpful way to navigate these situations is by using a decision tree: "Question: The government has passed a law that contradicts Jesus's teachings: do I comply? Answer: No, you seek a gracious way to dissent, following biblical examples of resistance."[34]

By studying these passages in context and applying their wisdom, the church is equipped to respond to political pressure in ways that honor God. This method helps ensure that Christians avoid falling into the trap of unconditional submission, instead remaining faithful to God's command, even when it leads them down uncomfortable or costly paths of resistance.

May we, like those who stood firm before us, find the courage to say "no" to the idols of our time, resolutely keeping our allegiance to Christ, the only true Lord, who calls us to bear witness to his kingdom of justice, peace, and love.

34. Hays, *Moral Vision of the New Testament.*

5.

Apartheid and the Body of Christ

IN A WORLD BROKEN by sin, injustice, and division, Jesus Christ calls his church to be ambassadors of healing, reconciliation, and unity, reflecting the heart and mission of God. The shadows of apartheid serve as a sobering reminder of how easily political and ideological actors can manipulate Christian faith to gain power.[1] Yet, the lessons from apartheid also invite us to stand firm in the truth of the gospel, where all are one in Christ, and no division can separate us from God's love.[2]

ALL ARE ONE IN CHRIST

The truth that all are one in Christ is the bedrock upon which the Christian faith stands, a proclamation that shatters the divisive powers of the world. When systemic evil threatens the church and world, such as apartheid or toxic forms of populism and Christian nationalism, this gospel-centered truth isn't merely a theological concept but God's call to the radical unity found in the body of Christ.

We've seen apartheid-like systems and practices in various parts of the world. Racist theologies and forms of Christian nationalism have often supported these. Examples include Australia (policies toward Indigenous Australians, including the Stolen Generations and racial segregation), Brazil (racial democracy myth vs. structural racism), China (Uighur

1. De Gruchy, *Church Struggle in South Africa.* For the use of Christian theology to support apartheid, see Villa-Vicencio, *Trapped in Apartheid.*

2. Gal 3:28 and Rom 8:38–39.

Muslims in Xinjiang), Colombia (discrimination against Afro-Colombians and Indigenous peoples), Guatemala (Indigenous marginalization), India (caste-based discrimination, particularly toward Dalits), Israel/Palestine (Israeli policies toward Palestinians within their state), Lebanon (sectarian discrimination and political segregation), Myanmar (discrimination and segregation of Rohingya Muslims), Namibia (under South African rule, racial segregation was enforced before independence), Nicaragua (segregation and marginalization of Indigenous populations), Rhodesia, which is now called Zimbabwe (racial segregation and white-minority rule before independence in 1980), and the United States (Jim Crow laws and racial segregation).

The apartheid system in South Africa (1948–1994) offers warnings and instructive narratives concerning how Christians should respond to political populism, Christian nationalism, and racist theologies and biblical interpretations.[3] Apartheid, as a regime founded on racial segregation and the belief in the superiority of one group over another, was a grievous affront to the gospel. The theology that justified the separation of people based on race betrayed the essence of Christian teaching: that all human beings, regardless of race or nationality, bear the image of God.

In response to the apartheid regime, faithful Christians clung to the truth that in Christ, God has created one new humanity (Eph 2:14–16). The theological rallying cry against apartheid's racial division was the biblical affirmation that there is neither Jew nor Greek, enslaved person nor free, male nor female, for all are one in Christ Jesus (Gal 3:28). This declaration was a direct challenge to the false doctrine that justified racial separation. It remains a stark reminder of the gospel's inherent opposition to racism. The church isn't an institution that serves the whims of nationalism or racial identity but is the body of Christ, a community that transcends the artificial divisions of the world.

The African independent churches and the mission churches during apartheid embodied this theological resistance. By holding multiracial prayer meetings and sharing communion (the Lord's Supper) across racial lines, they publicly defied the ideological boundaries that apartheid sought to establish. The Belhar Confession, written by the marginalized Dutch Reformed Mission Church in 1986, declared that unity and reconciliation

3. Villa-Vicencio, *Trapped in Apartheid.*

are at the heart of the gospel.[4] Any doctrine that sanctions racial division, it boldly stated, is a heresy.

For these dissenting, faithful Christians, the fight against apartheid wasn't merely a political struggle. The battle against the evils of racial segregation (a political system supported by Christian nationalistic theologies) was a profoundly spiritual confrontation rooted in the gospel's commitment to unity and equality before God. In this way, the confession became both a theological battering ram and a light of hope, challenging the entrenched powers of racial injustice with the radical love and reconciliation found in Christ.

GOD'S BIAS FOR JUSTICE AND THE CHURCH'S STAND WITH THE OPPRESSED

In a world where principalities and powers often integrate injustices, abuses, and oppression into the fabric of society, Jesus Christ calls his church to reject neutrality and stand with the oppressed. Under apartheid, the suffering of the black majority wasn't merely a social issue; it was a spiritual crisis that demanded a prophetic response from the church. Apartheid wasn't just a political system but a theological one that twisted Christian doctrine to justify inequality, violence, and systemic injustice. The state's use of Scripture, particularly passages like Rom 13, to legitimize apartheid was a blatant misapplication and misinterpretation of God's word. In response, South African Christians, grounded in faithful and robust engagements with the Bible, asserted that God isn't neutral in the face of oppression. God stands with the oppressed.

The Kairos Document, written by theologians of the apartheid era in 1985, provides a powerful theological manifesto for the church's response to injustice.[5] This document rejected the state's theology, which misused Scripture to sanctify apartheid. Instead, the authors called for a "prophetic theology" that would guide the church to resist the evil of oppression actively. The gospel isn't about passive submission to unjust rulers but about setting captives free, as Jesus proclaimed in his inaugural sermon in Luke 4:18. The church mustn't be passive but prophetic, not complicit but courageous, not abusive but apostolic, and not racist but reconciling: speaking

4. *Belhar Confession* (online).

5. *Kairos Document.*

against injustice and standing with those who suffer under systems of oppression.

This understanding of justice wasn't merely an abstract theological idea but a concrete call to action. Theologically, Christians understood that holiness isn't just personal piety but a commitment to social righteousness and that this conviction came with Christ's call to justice, mercy, compassion, righteousness, suffering, persecution, and even possible martyrdom. The Bible's call to "seek justice, correct oppression" (Isa 1:17) galvanized believers to view their anti-apartheid struggle not as political overreach but as an essential part of their discipleship. The Belhar Confession echoes this sentiment, stating that God has revealed Godself as the one who desires to bring about justice and peace among all people.[6] It calls the church to stand with the oppressed and to witness against any form of injustice actively. The Belhar Confession wasn't merely a theological statement but a clarion call to the church to live out its faith in a world broken by violence, hatred, division, oppression, abuses, and injustice. The kingdom of God requires Christians to be the opposite of those things: to be a people of peace, forgiveness, love, reconciliation, unity, liberation, healing, righteousness, and justice.

The church's role, according to the gospel, is to stand against oppression and fight for justice, not just in words but in actions. In this context, faith becomes inseparable from justice. To ignore the cries of the oppressed is to betray the very message of Christ, whose life, death, and resurrection were for the redemption of all people. As the church responds to injustice, it serves as a witness to the transformative power of the gospel, which calls not only for personal salvation but also for the healing and reconciliation of the world. Just as the South African church resisted the injustice of apartheid, so too are we called to resist the oppressive systems of our time and stand on the side of justice, mercy, and peace.

THE DUTCH REFORMED CHURCH'S SUPPORT OF APARTHEID THEOLOGY

The history of the Dutch Reformed Church (DRC) in South Africa serves as a poignant yet essential lesson about the church's capacity to be co-opted by ideologies that distort the gospel. In the early twentieth century, particularly in the 1930s and 1940s, influential theologians within the Dutch

6. *Belhar Confession* (online).

Reformed Church (DRC) crafted a theological framework to justify apartheid.[7] They misinterpreted key biblical narratives, such as the story of the Tower of Babel and the Curse of Ham, to claim that God had ordained separate races with distinct destinies.[8] This theological justification for racial segregation became deeply entrenched in the DRC's teaching, fueling the systemic oppression that would later define apartheid.

The DRC story reminds us always to check if what we believe aligns with what Jesus taught, or if we're letting other ideas sneak in that harm people. Ideologies that distort the gospel of Jesus Christ are always seeking to co-opt our imaginations and allegiances. They want to master our desires, visions, and actions. That should make us vigilant and cautious, leading us to examine our theological and moral convictions and resist becoming a tool for oppressive powers and principalities.

The DRC, as the dominant church among the Afrikaner population, held significant sway in society. It provided moral and theological cover for the apartheid regime, endorsing policies of racial segregation and white supremacy. Key decisions, like the 1857 synod's separation of communion for "the weakness of some," laid the groundwork for the later institutionalization of apartheid.[9] The DRC's theology not only affirmed apartheid but reinterpreted the gospel itself, distorting the biblical vision of unity and equality into a justification for racial division. The church was so powerful that it ended up supporting the government's terrible ideas about race, mixing their religious beliefs with harmful politics.

This alliance between the church and the state ultimately led to a tragic heresy. Instead of embracing the gospel's radical message of reconciliation and unity, the DRC's theology supported an ideological framework that perpetuated injustice. This isn't an isolated event in history, as similar patterns have emerged in other contexts where dominant groups have used theology to justify oppression. Just as "German Christians" in Nazi Germany twisted Christian doctrine to align with nationalist ideologies, the DRC's actions show how easily the church can fall into heresy when cultural supremacy dictates its theology.[10] Understanding this history challenges us today to examine where our churches may be vulnerable to similar

7. De Gruchy, *Church Struggle in South Africa.*

8. Bosch, *Transforming Mission.*

9. Pillay, *Religion at the Limits?*

10. Bergen, *Twisted Cross.*

distortions of the gospel. When the church aligns itself with the government in this manner, it loses its capacity to speak out against wrongdoings.

The church can't just follow the government if it's doing things that contradict the way of Christ. When we uncritically align ourselves with the state, we risk losing our prophetic voice, commitment to the Jesus Way, and dedication to being "salt, light, and a city on a hill."

THE BELHAR CONFESSION AND CHURCH RESISTANCE

In bold contrast to the theological distortions of the Dutch Reformed Church, the Belhar Confession stands as a courageous and unyielding declaration against apartheid, affirming the gospel's call to unity and justice. The Belhar Confession emerged in 1982 from the Reformed churches in South Africa, particularly the Dutch Reformed Mission Church, led by figures like Allan Boesak.[11] It declared apartheid to be not only a political evil but a heresy that undermined the very heart of the Christian faith. The Confession framed apartheid as a status issue, meaning that apartheid wasn't just a political problem but a direct challenge to the truth of the gospel.

The Belhar Confession stood up against apartheid and reminded everyone that the church should unite people, not divide them based on race. As Christians, we can't lose sight of our core mission to embody the inclusive, reconciling, just, countercultural love of Christ. Our values, habits, and lifestyles must transcend the borders, boundaries, divisions, and walls imposed by political and ideological powers, polarizations, and personalities.

The Belhar Confession's statement that "unity is, therefore, both a gift and an obligation for the church of Jesus Christ" boldly rejected the theological premise of apartheid, which sought to separate God's people along racial lines.[12] The Confession powerfully declared, "We reject any doctrine which absolutizes natural diversity or sinful separation of people such that it hinders unity." This was a revolutionary stance that rejected the apartheid system's claim that some people were inherently inferior and could be treated as second-class citizens.

This was a bold way of saying apartheid was wrong and that we can't let race separate us in the church. We're all one in Christ. Human differences

11. *Belhar Confession* (online).

12. *Belhar Confession* (online).

shouldn't lead to division. The gospel breaks down walls that separate us from each other.

This prophetic act of resistance wasn't just theoretical; it had real-world consequences. Many churches that refused to stand against apartheid or that continued to support it were expelled from the World Alliance of Reformed Churches.[13] But the Belhar Confession also became a source of hope and solidarity. It rallied Christians not only to resist the evil of apartheid but to embrace a higher calling: unity, reconciliation, and justice as core tenets of the gospel. The Confession offered a vision of the church as a community that transcended the artificial divisions of race and class, a community rooted in the love of Christ and committed to standing with the oppressed.

The church didn't just write profound things on paper; they stood up for unity and peace, even when it was dangerous to do so. They lived out their convictions even in the face of political violence, economic consequences, social backlash, religious insults, and institutionalized injustice.

The Confession's legacy is a powerful reminder that the church must never be silent in the face of injustice. Church leaders like Archbishop Desmond Tutu, who led peaceful protests and advocated for forgiveness and justice, embodied the message of the Belhar Confession.[14] Beyers Naudé, an Afrikaner pastor who broke from his Dutch Reformed Church (DRC) roots to join the struggle against apartheid, also reflected this commitment to resistance and reconciliation.[15]

The Belhar Confession tells us that the church should always speak out when something is wrong, even if it's hard or uncomfortable. We must be willing to speak prophetically against injustice and for the flourishing of all people, regardless of race, religion, politics, culture, gender, and socioeconomic status.

The Belhar Confession remains a unifying standard for churches in South Africa and around the world, a testament to the power of a church that refuses to compromise its allegiance to Christ in the face of oppressive power. This historical moment challenges us to examine whether we, too, are called to speak truth to power and proclaim a gospel of unity and justice in our own time. It's a reminder for us that the church can make a real difference by loving everyone equally and standing up for justice. We

13. De Gruchy, *Reconciliation.*

14. Tutu, *No Future Without Forgiveness.*

15. Villa-Vicencio, *Walk with Us and Listen.*

should seek to embody the gospel's call for equality, unity, reconciliation, and justice, too.

RACISM AS A GOSPEL ISSUE

The story of apartheid demands that we, as the church, wrestle with an irrefutable but often uncomfortable truth, which is that racism, in any form, stands in direct opposition to the gospel of Christ. When we tolerate or perpetuate racial divisions, we're not merely permitting social injustice; we're actively contradicting the message of Christ, who came to break down the walls that divide humanity. We must admit, without flinching, that racism is a sin. This sin seeks to dishonor the image of God in others and denies the unity we have in Christ.

The heart of the gospel is reconciliation. All forms of racism undermine the gospel. Racism tears apart what Jesus has united, leading us away from unity and compassion and toward division and hard-heartedness. We must look into our hearts and practices and root out all forms of racism.

The challenge today is for the church to examine its attitudes, structures, theologies, biblical interpretations, language, values, divisions, and practices. How often do we allow subtle prejudices to dictate our fellowship? How frequently do we ignore systemic exclusion or marginalization? Are we complicit in the sin of racism, whether passive or active? The church can't claim to follow Christ while harboring hatred or disdain toward any person made in God's image. Repentance mustn't be a one-time event; it's an ongoing, active commitment to transformation.

Our language, theologies, structures, and practices can easily reflect politics, prejudices, and ideologies instead of the truth of God's extravagant, inclusive, reconciling love. Are some people among us treated as inferior based on their social or financial status, gender, or ethnicity? How do we confront and change this situation?

Pastorally, the church must lead its people toward repentance. Such repentance isn't only for personal actions but also for the collective failures of the body of Christ in history. This must include confronting past complicity in the sins of slavery, segregation, hate speech, caste systems, and other forms of ethnic hatred. The church must create safe spaces for honest dialogue, guided by the example of South Africa's Truth and Reconciliation

Commission, where confession, lament, truth-telling, repentance, and forgiveness form the foundation of true healing.[16]

It's not enough to be sorry; we must change our actions, hearts, and communities. We must ensure that every individual feels equally valued within the fellowship of believers. The church's credibility rests on its ability to embody the love of Christ in a world rife with division. We can't claim to love God while harboring hatred toward our neighbor. Forgiveness and reconciliation are the heart of discipleship and the gospel, and it demands that we work tirelessly to root out racism in all its forms.

RECONCILIATION AND JUSTICE AS A CONTINUOUS JOURNEY

Reconciliation, as the South African church's experience shows, isn't a quick or easy path; it's a continuous journey requiring both dedication and endurance.[17] Forgiveness, though essential, isn't the end of the story. It must be coupled with tangible acts of justice. These acts must address the wrongs done, seek to repair the harm caused, involve the leadership of those who've suffered, and work toward healing.

We never arrive at reconciliation as a fixed destination. Reconciliation is a process and journey, a path we're continually on. This narrow, difficult path requires integrity, repentance, lament, humility, courage, truth-telling, and constant effort to replace injustice and wrongs with God's holy, restorative truth, love, and shalom (restoring things to God's original good intent). Reconciliation requires changing hearts and also addressing power structures.

As Christians, we can't settle for the illusion of peace while injustice continues to flourish. Reconciliation requires truth-telling, lament, and the courageous confrontation of systems and structures of oppression and injustice. True reconciliation involves the hard work of righting the wrongs of the past, which may include restitution, the restoration of stolen land, and the correction of long-standing inequalities.[18] The spiritual call to forgiveness isn't a soft, passive call; it's a prophetic call that demands courageous, humble, Christlike action and change. Churches can't shy away from

16. Tutu, *No Future Without Forgiveness.*

17. De Gruchy, *Reconciliation.*

18. Villa-Vicencio, *Walk with Us and Listen.*

confronting the root causes of division, racism, sexism, inequality, poverty, oppression, and systemic injustice.

In pastoral practice, this means we must challenge the church to embrace a holistic view of justice. Such a biblical view of justice integrates both forgiveness and practical action, reflecting the words and actions of the prophets, apostles, and Jesus Christ. Many South African churches used Mic 6:8 as their guiding verse: "What does the Lord require of you? To act justly, love mercy, and walk humbly with your God." This verse remains an enduring call for all Christians not only to seek personal holiness but also to act in ways that promote justice, righteousness, love, humility, compassion, and mercy in the world around us. For those who are pastors, teachers, and ministers, we can't be content with merely preaching personal holiness: we must also exhort our congregations to acknowledge and stand against injustices and systems of oppression and act for a better, more Christ-honoring and God-glorifying church and world.

Faith isn't merely a private matter but is meant to be expressed in how we engage with the world, particularly with those who have been marginalized, exploited, abused, and oppressed. We must look at the injustices around us (whether racial inequality, economic injustice, or any form of exclusion) and ask ourselves: "What are we doing to stand with those who are treated as 'less than'?"

The work of reconciliation is never finished. We must always ask how we can help bring justice and healing to those on the margins. This journey demands perseverance, humility, commitment, and sacrifice. Are we willing to commit to the long, slow work of rebuilding communities and relationships? Just as the church in South Africa has continued to address issues like poverty, racial divisions, inequalities, and AIDS, we, too, must commit to a long obedience in the same direction, which brings justice, healing, and restoration to all people.[19]

UNITY IN WORSHIP AND PRACTICING INCLUSION

In the wake of apartheid, many courageous Christians in South Africa, despite the law, militias, and threats, gathered in defiance of the regime's hatred and discrimination, uniting across racial lines in acts of worship that boldly declared God's vision for the world: a vision of unity and reconciliation

19. Peterson, *Long Obedience in the Same Direction.*

in Jesus Christ.[20] These multiracial services weren't just acts of defiance; they were profound spiritual practices, uniting people of different ethnicities and backgrounds into a singular community, celebrating their unity in their differences and diversity, woven together by Christ. This practice wasn't merely symbolic but a clear demonstration of what God's kingdom values and looks like, where there is no separation, division, discrimination, or exclusion. The church, in these moments, embodied the truth that in Christ, all are one (Gal 3:28).

This call to unity in worship is a practice we must continue to embrace today, especially in a world increasingly gripped by divisions of race, class, age, ability, politics, gender, culture, and identity. Church communities can begin to intentionally create spaces where all voices are heard, where people of diverse backgrounds lead, and where the richness of varied cultural expressions is enjoyed in our worship. One practice is the incorporation of hymns and songs from different cultures and languages. These songs, sung in unity, not only celebrate diversity but also reaffirm our shared faith in unity. Another practice might be alternating leadership roles in worship, inviting people from diverse ethnicities and age groups to lead and serve, thereby demonstrating that all are welcome to participate in the body of Christ.

A "Galatians 3:28 Sunday" might serve as an annual or seasonal occasion to highlight this unity, where church leaders of diverse ethnicities co-preach and share the word together (potentially in a TED-talk style, dialogical model, integrated joint sermon, or symbolic co-preaching format). Such unified and shared preaching and teaching is a visual declaration that Christ's gospel transcends all earthly divisions. As we learn about one another's stories (especially those of race, class, socioeconomic status, ethnicity, and cultural experience), we practice empathy. We grow in understanding and begin to dismantle unconscious biases that keep us separated. Much like the moving and costly acts of reconciliation seen in South Africa, where people washed each other's feet in a tangible act of humility and mutual respect, modern churches can adopt similar rituals that promote healing and unity. These practices align our hearts with the profound, spiritual reality that, in Christ, we are truly one.

Through worship and communal acts of inclusion, the church becomes a powerful antidote to divisive ideologies like apartheid and radical nationalism. Churches no longer remain passive institutions but become

20. De Gruchy, *Church Struggle in South Africa*.

vibrant communities and witnesses to the world that there is neither Jew nor Greek, enslaved nor free, progressive nor conservative, Republican nor Democrat, immigrant nor native-born, but all are one in Christ. By living out this unity, we help inoculate our communities against the subtle forces of division and exclusion, countering hatred with love and separation with unity in Christ.

PRAYING WITH THE OPPRESSED

When we witness injustice or hear the cries of the exploited, silenced, and oppressed, our first response as Christians isn't just to feel sorrow but to pray. Like the Psalmist, our songs and prayers can arise from our laments and grief and be instrumental in our change and transformation. This practice of intercessory prayer is a powerful way to spiritually stand with the suffering, to "bear one another's burdens" (Gal 6:2). Theologians, mystics, and saints have long understood that prayer isn't a passive act; it's an active form of solidarity. Contemplation, action, and solidarity are integral to each other's vitality and integrity. Through prayer, we identify with those who suffer, not by merely sympathizing but by stepping into their pain, entering into the ache that they carry, and lifting them before God's throne of grace.

In the context of modern struggles, Jesus Christ calls us to pray for those who are downtrodden, vulnerable, and suffering, whether they face racial violence, economic injustice, displacement, or marginalization. One way to deepen this practice is to choose a specific group or situation and dedicate ourselves to praying for them on a regular basis. During the apartheid era, Christians worldwide prayed fervently for South Africa, asking God to bring peace, justice, liberation, and conversion. In the same way, we can bring before God those suffering today, asking for the Spirit's intervention in situations like ethnic conflicts, refugee crises, impoverished rural and urban communities, the epidemic of addictions, and systemic racial injustice.

Such prayers can be guided by Scripture, using the words of the Psalms or Mary's Magnificat, which exalts the humble and brings down the proud (Luke 1:46–55). The Psalms provide a voice for the cries of the oppressed, making them an apt tool for lament and intercession. Additionally, prayer can be enriched by fasting, which is an act of self-denial that aligns our hearts with the pain of the marginalized and the passion and purposes of

God. By fasting or simplifying our own lives, we engage in a spiritual solidarity that compels us to act in ways that align with God's justice.

But intercessory prayer does more than connect us to the suffering of others; it reshapes us. As we intercede for those who suffer, God enlarges our compassion, sharpening our sense of God's righteous anger against injustice and deepening our longing for reconciliation. When we pray with the oppressed, we allow their suffering to become our own, and we stand with them in the face of injustice. This practice guards us against apathy and indifference, ensuring that the issues of justice aren't "out there" somewhere but are deeply intertwined with our faith. It's in these moments that we align ourselves with God's will for God's world: to bring healing, peace, freedom, dignity, and justice to the shamed and broken.

As we learn to pray in solidarity with the oppressed, we follow in the footsteps of Christ, who humbled and emptied himself for our sake, identifying fully with the marginalized, shamed, and outcast (Phil 2:5–8). Through our prayers, we participate in God's ongoing work of reconciliation, seeking not only spiritual healing but tangible justice for the world's wounded.

CHURCH PRONOUNCEMENTS AND CONFESSIONS AND CREEDS AS GUIDES

Our world is saturated by ever-shifting political ideologies and social movements. In this contested context, God has given the church a timeless gift: the clarity of shared wisdom expressed in confessions, declarations, Scripture, and creeds. I recall when my daughter was young, hearing her walking around our house singing "This I Believe" (the Apostles' Creed).[21] She was singing the core of Christian belief, and I'm sure it was sinking deep into her heart, mind, and desires. The Apostles' Creed is a bold declaration of the most wonderful truth in the universe: the story of God and our Lord Jesus Christ that will save and transform the heavens and the earth. Any political, philosophical, or social ideology that claims a supreme understanding of the truth is exposed as a lie in the light of the truth of the gospel of Jesus Christ, expressed in the Christian Scriptures and historical creeds.

Just as South African Christians courageously drafted the Belhar Confession in the face of apartheid's evils, churches today can draw from both the historical Christian creeds and other foundational confessions to guide

21. Hillsong, "This I Believe (The Creed)."

their discernment.[22] The Belhar Confession, rooted in the gospel's call for unity and justice, stands as a potent reminder that God's kingdom transcends the boundaries of race, politics, ideology, nationality, and power. When faced with moral confusion and political pressure, we can turn to similar documents (such as the Cape Town Commitment or the prophetic words of Martin Luther King Jr. in his "Letter from Birmingham Jail") to gain clarity about our response and help us navigate difficult or perilous times.[23]

The church's collective wisdom, shaped by years of struggle, provides a lens through which to evaluate the moral integrity of contemporary political claims. When national leaders or popular ideologies promote division or injustice, believers must hold those claims up against the truths enshrined in our faith. Suppose a political platform claims divine sanction for separating people or justifying inequality. In that case, we must reject it outright, not as a matter of opinion, but as a matter of theological integrity. The church's pronouncements, birthed from the furnace of struggle, speak with the weight of history and faith, urging us to measure all claims against God's kingdom.

When we hear rhetoric that elevates one group over another, claiming divine exclusivity, we can recall the Belhar Confession's rejection of "separate but equal" as a perversion of the gospel. We're blessed to have Scripture and Creed to guide us. We can also turn to the collective wisdom of the global church, embodied in its confessions and declarations. These help us ground our discernment and decision-making in shared Christian convictions rather than being clouded by personal, partisan, or cultural biases.

IMAGO DEI LITMUS TEST

Genesis 1:26–27 tells us that people are made in the *imago Dei* (the "image of God"). "Then God said, 'Let us make humanity in our image, in our likeness, so that they may rule over the fish in the sea and the birds in the sky, over the livestock and all the wild animals, and over all the creatures that move along the ground.' So, God created humanity in God's own image, in the image of God they were created, male and female God created them."[24]

22. *Belhar Confession* (online).

23. Bock, *Cape Town Commitment*; King, "Letter from a Birmingham Jail."

24. Genesis 1:26–27 paraphrased by me to ensure gender-neutral language.

Since God created people in his image, all people are precious and imbued with inherent dignity, worth, and purpose. All are equal in God's eyes, a truth that levels hierarchies based on gender, class, race, wealth, language, culture, politics, or power. We must respect and honor others as they are created in God's image, showing all people love and understanding and noticing the spark of the divine within them. Lucy Peppiatt says, "To have been created intentionally, imagined in the mind of God, and then brought into being communicates something profound about a person's intrinsic worth. It speaks: you are loved; you are wanted; you are valued. Further to this, to have been created as some kind of reflection or embodiment of the divine serves only to strengthen the idea that human beings are of infinite worth and beauty."[25]

At the heart of the Christian response to political ideologies is a profound theological question: Does this affirm the image of God in all people, or does it deny it? The doctrine of the *imago Dei* (the belief that every person is made in the image of God) was an essential truth trampled upon during apartheid, as entire communities were reduced to less than human. This test, rooted in Gen 1, serves as a robust measure for discerning whether any social or political stance aligns with God's truth.

Today, when we encounter divisive rhetoric or discriminatory policies, we must ask: Does this view uphold the dignity of all people, or does it dehumanize them? If a particular group is depicted as inferior, dangerous, or irredeemable, we know immediately that it fails the *imago Dei* test. If a policy places one group's rights above others, it, too, falls short of God's justice. On the other hand, actions that affirm the worth of every individual and seek the flourishing of all align with God's vision of a just and compassionate world. When a political discourse dehumanizes people of color or vilifies refugees and immigrants, it utterly fails the *imago Dei* test. Conversely, when a proposal seeks to provide education and opportunity to historically marginalized groups, it honors the image of God in all people.

This profound yet straightforward litmus test forces us to cut through the noise of political rhetoric and see the deeper truth of human dignity. It calls us to reject ideological positions that degrade or exclude while embracing those that reflect the love and justice of Christ. Just as South African Christians eventually came to see their black neighbors as brothers and sisters, the *imago Dei* test compels us to recognize the humanity of all people, regardless of their background or status. In doing so, we allow our

25. Peppiatt, *Imago Dei*, 139.

political actions to be shaped by love, compassion, and justice, ensuring that our witness aligns with the gospel's call to equality before God.

As the Spirit of Christ moves upon our hearts and imaginations, let's pause and reflect on the image of God in each person. The *imago Dei* invites us not only to see the beauty and holiness of God's presence in all people but also to love, honor, and restore what has been fractured.

6.

Kingdom Citizens in Public Life

As followers of Jesus Christ, we are citizens of two realms: the kingdom of God and the societies in which we live. Our world is saturated in political chaos, competing ideologies and interests, and cultural fragmentation. When we practice the way of Jesus, we can't withdraw in fear or seek to dominate through power and control. Instead, Jesus calls us to embody the values of God's kingdom right in every cultural and social context we're in. Our public lives aren't mere transactions or political affiliations; they're sacred vocations, where the witness of our lives speaks louder than any platform, performance, politics, or party. We live as pilgrims, ambassadors, and servants, seeking the welfare of our communities while remaining steadfast to the rule and reign of Jesus Christ our Lord.

PILGRIMS AND AMBASSADORS

As we consider the loyalties Christians juggle, we can describe followers of Jesus as dual citizens inhabiting two realms: the kingdom of God and the earthly communities where we live. This dual citizenship creates uncomfortable tensions and necessitates careful decision-making. We are in the world, yet not of it. We belong to a higher calling, a kingdom that transcends borders, walls, cultures, nations, races, ideologies, and political systems. Yet, we must still engage with the broken realities of our world. That's hard to do, so it's always easier to fall in line with the thinking of political or national interests. But the Bible reminds us that we're pilgrims passing through, yet ambassadors with a mandate to represent Christ wherever we find ourselves.

As pilgrims, we travel lightly, go where the Spirit leads, and never fully settle, for our hope is in a future that's yet to come. But as ambassadors, we carry the full weight of Christ's kingdom (its truth, mercy, and justice), practice the Jesus Way in culturally and socially sensitive practices, and seek to proclaim the lordship and shalom of Jesus Christ into the places he sends us.

In his prayer for his disciples in John 17, Jesus implored the Father to protect them as they remained in the world.[1] But this wasn't a prayer for their isolation, retreat, or withdrawal. Instead, it was Christ's call to faithful presence in a world marked by evil, suffering, longing, and often a desire for a better world.[2] Jesus calls us to be "salt and light" (Matt 5:13–16), shaping the world without allowing it to shape us. Our engagement isn't one of conquest or withdrawal but faithful influence.

As Christians, our public life is an extension of our discipleship. In every realm (political, cultural, personal, and social), we are to be agents of reconciliation, truth, shalom, and grace. Our lives bear witness to the one who was both a pilgrim on earth and the ultimate ambassador of the kingdom of heaven. In this journey, our influence should never be about power for power's sake but about sacrifice, humility, and a commitment to serve.

PROPHETS AND PRIESTS

God has given the church a unique role in society: that of prophet and priest. Prophets speak truth to power. Priests embody mercy, compassion, and care for those in need. Jesus was both a prophetic voice that confronted injustice with holy passion and a high priest who bore our burdens. He compels us to follow his example, living out this balance through our discipleship in the world.

The prophets of old, such as Nathan, Jeremiah, Isaiah, Elijah, and Amos, didn't hesitate to confront the political powers of their day with the truth of God's justice.[3] They stood up when others hid away, spoke out when others were silent, and paid a high cost for their courage when doing

1. John 17:14–18.

2. Hunter, *To Change the World*; Taylor, "Changing the World Through Faithful Presence."

3. Jer 1:10; 2 Sam 12:7–10; Isa 1:10–17; Amos 5:21–24.

and saying nothing would have been easier. The prophets called kings and rulers to account, and they proclaimed the coming kingdom of God that would set all things right. The priestly role, however, isn't one of confrontation but of intercession and care. Priests in the Old Testament mediated between God and God's people, offering sacrifices and prayers on behalf of the people.[4] Christ calls his church to embody both of these roles: speaking truth boldly yet also offering care and mercy to the broken, suffering, impoverished, and marginalized.

This calling isn't simply theoretical; it's deeply practical, worked out in our everyday lives and relationships. A prophetic church speaks out against injustice, but it also offers tangible acts of mercy. It might be the church that runs a soup kitchen, providing for the daily needs of those experiencing poverty while also campaigning for affordable housing and advocating for justice in the systems that perpetuate poverty and marginalization. It might be the church that speaks up for working-class people who've been left behind by globalization and technology, advocating for those whose communities have been decimated by global forces they have no control over. It may also be the church that provides refuge for those whom immigration would rip from their families and deport into dangerous environments. A prophetic choice can speak and act on behalf of all people, regardless of their race, immigration status, political persuasion, social class, or urban or rural setting. In this way, the prophetic and the priestly aren't separate endeavors but are bound together in Christlike love.

The church doesn't exist to serve any political party, nationalistic or populist interest, or ideology; it exists to bear witness to the kingdom of God revealed in Christ Jesus. This kingdom is characterized by truth, righteousness, humility, service, justice, mercy, peace, and the fruit of the Spirit. This isn't a political mission but a sacred vocation that doesn't belong to any earthly kingdom but to the kingdom of God alone.

By framing the church's public witness in these prophetic and priestly terms, we're reminded that our engagement with the world must never be dominated by partisanship or by populist and nationalistic interests. Our actions are rooted in the kingdom of God, not in any earthly political agenda. N. T. Wright has suggested that the church is a small working model of the new creation.[5] Jesus calls us to live as if God's kingdom is already here (because it is among us), bearing witness to the transformative power

4. Lev 4:20; Lev 16:15–19.

5. Wright, *After You Believe*.

of the gospel through words, signs, and deeds. When the church embodies its prophetic and priestly role, it becomes a true sign of what God has promised to do for the world: to bring justice, reconciliation, and renewal to all things.

UNITED STATES CHURCHES AMID POLITICAL POLARIZATION

Let's turn to the United States for some case studies in faithfulness amid political pressures. In recent years, many expressions of American Christianity have become increasingly entangled with political polarization, creating a deep rift within the church. The sharp divide between left and right hasn't only reshaped public discourse but has also infiltrated the church, leaving it torn between partisan ideologies and the gospel of Christ. Some evangelical leaders have become closely aligned with political movements, wielding their pulpits as platforms for partisan rhetoric. This entanglement with political power has led to a dangerous conflation of faith with political identity, compromising the church's witness to a watching world.

Yet, in the midst of this, voices are rising to challenge this trend. Movements like the *& Campaign* urge Christians to remain "politically homeless," seeking to transcend the divisiveness of the culture wars and reaffirm their allegiance to Christ alone.[6] These voices call Christians to reflect on their primary identity, not as partisans but as citizens of the kingdom of God.

In this polarized context, some pastors have taken courageous steps to disentangle the church from political power. In a bold rejection of unhealthy nationalism, particular churches have removed national flags from their sanctuaries, choosing instead to place Christ at the center of their worship. Preaching through a series on the kingdom of God, they aim to correct the narrative that has associated faith with a single political party. Tim Keller, among others, has cautioned Christians not to tether their faith to any political platform, urging a more biblically balanced approach to public engagement.[7]

So, what are some other examples of American churches and groups seeking to nurture a nonpartisan approach to faith during polarized times?

6. The AND Campaign, *Compassion (&) Conviction*.

7. Keller, *Center Church*.

The Evangelical Covenant Church encourages members to avoid political partisanship, emphasizing the church's unity in Christ over political division. The Christian Community Development Association (CCDA) emphasizes social justice and community transformation while maintaining a nonpartisan stance in its efforts.

The National Association of Evangelicals (NAE) advocates for unity and a nonpartisan approach to public engagement, prioritizing the gospel's message over partisan ideologies. The Anabaptist network calls Christians to reject political alliances and instead focus on discipleship and the kingdom of God.

The Vineyard movement advocates for engaging public life through love and justice without being defined by political ideologies. The Roman Catholic Church's social teaching encourages nonpartisan political engagement, emphasizing care for the marginalized and justice over any particular political agenda. The Anglican Church in North America (ACNA) prioritizes the gospel's call to justice and reconciliation over political entanglements.

New Monastic Communities (e.g., The Simple Way) focus on living out the gospel through community, justice, and reconciliation without being co-opted by political movements. The Salvation Army prioritizes social justice and service to marginalized communities, maintaining a nonpartisan approach in its work. Christians for Social Action promotes a nonpartisan approach to social justice, advocating for a biblical engagement with the public sphere that prioritizes compassion and justice.[8]

The good news is that we can find many examples. Sure, they do it imperfectly since all organizations struggle to live out their ideals, but they are giving nonpartisan gospel faithfulness a go in politically partisan times.

There's a genuine cost of conflating faith with politics, especially in moments like the events surrounding January 6, 2021, when the church's witness was damaged by political allegiance.[9] Yet, we see hopeful examples of churches striving to maintain unity in Christ, placing the gospel above political identity. These stories provide a powerful model for churches today, showing that in times of division, our call isn't to power but to the faithful presence of Christ in the world.

Amid the storms of populism and politics, an untamed, wild, Christ-like revolution is happening. Not the kind that seizes power or grabs

8. Christians for Social Action, "Our Mission and Vision."

9. Wehner, "Evangelical Church Is Breaking Apart."

headlines, but a revolution in the hearts of believers who refuse to bow to the false idols of partisan allegiance. These are the quiet warriors (pastors, poets, prophets, leaders, and communities) standing firm in their resolve to witness to a kingdom that is not of this world. In this kingdom, the dividing lines of politics and power are swallowed up by the unrelenting flood of Christ's love. Their journey isn't one of easy triumph, nor is it without cost, struggle, fear, and pain. The wounds of a divided church bleed through the pews, but from these wounds, there rises a call to unity. Churches that remove the national flag to elevate the cross above all aren't just making symbolic gestures; they're saying, with humble conviction, "We choose the Lamb over the donkey and elephant." The gospel, they say, isn't a tool to secure earthly dominion but a living testimony to a kingdom where mercy, justice, service, humility, sacrifice, inclusion, and love are the currency and where every partisan divide is laid bare by the cross of Christ.

THE CHURCH AS PEACEMAKER IN THE MAJORITY WORLD

While political polarization has caused deep fractures in the church in the West, the global church offers compelling examples of how to navigate public life with reconciliation and peace-making at the forefront.

In Myanmar, where the winds of political unrest whip the land, the church has risen, not as a fortress of refuge but as a lighthouse, its flickering light cutting through the storm of division. Amid the cacophony of ethnic strife and governmental strangleholds, Christian voices (both Catholic and Protestant) have pursued dialogue, not as mere words, but as lifelines. With hearts held together by a gospel of reconciliation, they've dared to speak across the trenches of war, calling not for the sharp edge of violence but for the gentle hands of nonviolent resolution. They've opened their doors wide to the displaced, offering not just shelter but space for broken hearts to heal and for fragmented lives to be reknit. In a society fractured by fear and suspicion, the church's presence has been a compass, pointing not to power or politics, but to something far more ancient: a way of peace that transcends borders or parties, bound by a kingdom that surpasses them all.

In South Sudan, the church emerged as a moral voice amid one of the most brutal civil wars in recent memory.[10] After the country's independence, the conflict between the Dinka and Nuer ethnic groups spiraled

10. Ashworth, *Voice of the Voiceless.*

into violence, with politicians and militias further fueling the divide. But Christian leaders across Catholic, Anglican, and other traditions answered a higher calling: to be peacemakers. By hosting dialogues and prayer meetings, they managed to bring both sides together when political leaders failed to find common ground. These church leaders embodied Jesus's beatitude "Blessed are the peacemakers," serving as a moral compass for their society amid ethnic and political chaos.

In Colombia, churches played a pivotal role in facilitating peace during the FARC insurgency. Christian leaders from both Protestant and Catholic traditions took an active role in reconciling warring factions. Through prayer meetings and reconciliation ceremonies, they became the trusted bridge between government and guerrilla fighters. In a landscape torn apart by violence, the church's prophetic voice for justice and forgiveness offered an alternative path forward, demonstrating to the world that peace is possible through Christ.

Similarly, in the Solomon Islands, churches became intermediaries amid ethnic conflict. With rival tribal groups at odds, Christian leaders from various denominations led reconciliation efforts, offering both spiritual healing and practical dialogue to foster unity. Churches have provided spaces for open communication and forgiveness between groups that have historically been at odds, embodying the truth that the church should always stand as an agent of peace.

In Lebanon, the church has been at the forefront of peacebuilding efforts since the end of the Lebanese Civil War, working across sectarian lines to foster unity. Christian leaders, despite their denominational differences, have united in calling for national healing. They have organized interfaith dialogues, providing a platform for religious leaders to collaborate for peace, justice, and societal renewal. The church's role here as a peacemaker transcends mere political alignment; it's a testimony to the kingdom of God that brings hope and unity to a deeply divided society.

Finally, in Ukraine, as the nation faces the tension of ongoing conflict with Russia, the church is once again rising to fulfill its role as the moral heart of society.[11] Orthodox, Catholic, and Protestant leaders have united in a spirit of resistance to division, offering humanitarian aid, organizing prayer services, and calling for justice and peace. Their message has transcended political boundaries, offering a vision of the kingdom where

11. Mandaville, *Geopolitics of Religious Soft Power.*

Christ's love and compassion reign supreme, even in the darkest times of conflict.

By resisting the lure of factional power, the church becomes a powerful force for the common good, offering the world a glimpse of Christ's kingdom, where justice, peace, and mercy reign. These stories aren't just historical; they resonate with the present challenges we face in a world torn by division.

Amid the noise of politics (loud, shrill, relentless), where the church in the West often stands divided by the fractures of party lines, the global church offers a different melody. It sings of peace, as an abstract dream, but as a living, breathing force. They are the marks of the body of Christ living out the very essence of its calling. The church, across oceans, across cultures, is a scandal to the world: a testament to the unrelenting truth that in Christ, there is no longer division, no longer us versus them. There's only the invitation to God's surprising, diverse, expansive banquet table, where even the most broken lives are offered joy and wholeness, even in the midst of chaos.

As we look to the global church for guidance, we learn that Christlike presence in public life isn't about aligning with earthly powers but about transforming them through love, compassion, justice, and reconciliation. This vision of the church offers a compelling alternative to the political idolatry that dominates much of the public sphere in the West.

RESISTING POLITICAL IDOLATRY

Political polarization and extremism are on the rise, and Christians must resist the idols of power, division, and ideology. The first commandment presents a resounding challenge to every Christian heart: "You shall have no other gods before me."[12] This isn't just a question of personal idolatry but a call to examine how political allegiance can become an idol, displacing our loyalty to Christ.

When political ideologies (whether left or right, conservative or progressive, or whatever stripe) begin to demand our unwavering devotion, we must ask, "Have I allowed the Elephant or Donkey to take the place of the Lamb? Am I following the beasts of ideology, nationalism, and political populism rather than the Lion of Judah? Have I been dragged into the culture wars and their never-ending desire to conquer their opponents

12. Exod 20:3.

instead of imitating the humble, reconciling, suffering Servant?" Ideologies that absolutize personal freedom, elevating individual autonomy above the collective call to love one's neighbor, directly contradict Christ's teachings. Equally, those who idolize state power and authority risk undermining the sacred roles of the church and the family as outlined in Scripture. Political platforms aren't the kingdom of God, and they offer manifold idols that threaten our allegiance and worship of the one true God.

No earthly system can bear the weight of divine truth, and the church must resist any temptation to reduce the kingdom of God to any earthly ideology. Augustine's notion of *ordo amoris* teaches that when love for a cause, ideology, personality, party, nation, culture, ethnic group, or power displaces love for God, it becomes idolatry, distorting our identity and leading to the perils of nationalism and populism, where earthly allegiances are elevated above the divine order.[13] The Spirit of Christ invites us to evaluate where political parties align with, or depart from, Christian values and to speak truth courageously, even if it means standing apart from political factions.

In doing so, we not only maintain our fidelity to Christ but also offer the world a stark, necessary reminder that our allegiance is always to the Lamb, not the party.

CIVILITY AND LOVE

Vitriol, accusations, incivility, and division mar a significant portion of public discourse today, particularly in established, new, and social media spaces. In this environment, followers of Jesus must recognize that our tone is just as important as our message. To speak truth is to speak in love; to engage with others is to do so with humility, patience, respect, and a desire to understand and empathize. The world is watching, and it sees more clearly the manner of our witness than the content of our message.

Too often, Christians have fallen prey to the same polarizing rhetoric that has come to define our times, using the same tools of division and hostility in the name of Christ. We get involved in online arguments, scapegoat certain groups, caricature the positions and beliefs of others, diminish the perspectives and experiences of our opponents, and allow ourselves to be drawn into the ugly social media culture wars. Yet the very nature of the kingdom we proclaim demands a different way: a way of civility, respect,

13. Augustine, *City of God* 19.13–14.

and love that mirrors the gentleness of Christ (and the whole fruit of the Spirit). Paul exhorts the church to "speak the truth in love" and to be ready to answer "with gentleness and respect."[14] This isn't a call to compromise on truth but a demand to uphold truth in a spirit of grace.

If our convictions drive us to slander, vilify, or belittle those who oppose us, then we've lost the essence of Christ's love and are no longer following the Jesus Way. Instead, Christ calls us to overcome evil with good, to bless those who curse us, and to pray for those who persecute us.[15] Such behavior flows from the fruit of the Spirit, the very qualities that should characterize every Christian: patience, kindness, gentleness, and self-control.[16] These virtues aren't mere politeness but the manifestation of holiness.

If we hope to engage culture in a way that honors Christ, we must resist the allure of populist outrage and embrace a more Christlike engagement that calls for not just correct beliefs but a proper manner of living those beliefs out in the public square. As Richard Mouw has suggested, we must practice "uncommon decency" in our political engagement, not only for the sake of our consciences but as a witness to the watching world.[17]

PRACTICALLY NURTURING THE SPIRITUALITY OF JESUS

Our local churches have a profound opportunity and responsibility to be living alternatives to the nationalism, populism, and political idolatry that so often dominate public life. To express the spirituality of Jesus, we must become communities that embody his radical way of love, justice, peace, and self-giving service. In the face of coercion, we offer compassion. In a world divided by tribalism, we extend grace. Where there's injustice, we uphold the passions of our just God. When polarization and division threaten relationships and harmony, we practice the ministry of reconciliation and the radical, self-giving, costly love of Jesus Christ.

The countercultural spirituality of Jesus calls us to live cross-shaped lives that subvert the empire's values of power, control, grasping, wall-building, and division and reflect the heart of Christ. Churches can cultivate this

14. Eph 4:15; 1 Pet 3:15.

15. Rom 12:21; Matt 5:44.

16. Gal 5:22–23.

17. Mouw, *Uncommon Decency*.

spirituality by engaging in practices that remind us of Jesus's kingdom: a kingdom of humility, service, reconciliation, shalom, justice, righteousness, kindness, mercy, hope, and love.

One of the most effective ways a local church can nurture this spirituality is through communal worship that centers on Christ rather than on national symbols or political ideologies. The Eucharist itself, the Table of Jesus, is a subversive act: a declaration that the kingdom of God is where all are equal, where political boundaries are dissolved, and where the least are welcomed.[18] By consistently preaching a gospel that emphasizes the reign of God over every earthly authority, the church helps its members see their true allegiance. This means that worship must include reflection on Jesus's life, his refusal of worldly power, and his radical inclusion of those marginalized by society. As a church, the liturgy becomes a place where the values of the kingdom are lived out in truth, love, and unity, transcending political divides.

Our churches can offer alternative models of justice and peacemaking. Jesus's call to love our enemies, welcome strangers, care for foreigners and immigrants, seek the well-being of those left behind by institutions and powers (such as working-class people and others suffering due to globalization and technologies), seek peace, and do justice isn't just a nice idea but a radical call to action. Local churches can embody this through advocacy for the oppressed, standing up for the rights of impoverished and forgotten working classes and ethnicities, involvement in interfaith dialogues, and organizing peace-building events that create spaces for healing and reconciliation.

In these practices, Christians reject the false narratives of division and hostility that characterize much of the political landscape and instead embody the gospel of reconciliation that Jesus demonstrated on the cross. Our churches can be lighthouses of faith, hope, and love for both those that progressives often advocate for (such as marginalized minorities and immigrants) and conservatives rightly say society has too frequently forgotten (such as impoverished and struggling working-class and rural or regional communities). Practicing the spirituality and gospel of Jesus means being beacons of compassion and hope for all those Jesus Christ died for, and that means everyone, regardless of religion, class, race, politics, gender, and so forth.

18. Wright, *Meal Jesus Gave Us*.

Jesus's radical love and gospel of salvation and hope are for all people, so our churches must be for all people, too, showing the world that we follow Jesus in dismantling divisions and offering reconciliation and the fullness of life in God.

THE JESUS WAY AS A RADICAL DISCIPLESHIP THAT SUBVERTS EMPIRE

The term "the Way," used to describe early Christians in Acts 9:1–4, is a profound and radical declaration of what it means to follow Jesus.[19] The Jesus Way isn't merely about personal salvation; it's a comprehensive life that resists the forces of empire, power, and division. It's a way that demands radical discipleship, where believers are marked not by their allegiance to political ideologies but by their commitment to Christ's teachings of love, humility, and justice.

The Jesus Way calls us to reject self-interest and embrace a life of compassion and peace. This Way means that the local church must teach and live a spirituality of radical generosity, where resources are shared, where the impoverished and marginalized are cared for, and where the rights of others are upheld as sacred. In the Jesus Way, there's no room for the accumulation of power or wealth at the expense of others. Instead, Jesus calls his followers to embody justice, not as a political tool, but as the will of God for all people.

Living the Jesus Way also means embracing the rhythm of prayer and communion with God, which shapes a posture of humility and dependence. It's in prayer that God reminds Christians of their true citizenship in the kingdom of God and their call to resist the temptation to conform to the values of earthly kingdoms. Through prayer, the church is united not around a political agenda but around the shared mission of embodying Christ's love and truth in a world torn by division. By fostering communities rooted in prayer, compassion, and justice, the church becomes a living testament to the alternative kingdom that Jesus proclaimed.[20] This kingdom is one where Christ's peace, truth, and divine love reign, offering a compelling vision of the world as it ought to be.

19. Gorman, *Becoming the Gospel.*

20. Peterson, *Christ Plays in Ten Thousand Places.*

"WHAT WOULD JESUS HAVE ME DO?"

It seems like yesterday when many Christians were wearing WWJD (What Would Jesus Do?) bracelets. The trend has faded, but imitating Christ must never cease. In a fractured and polarized world, Christians must find creative ways to imitate and conform to the example of Jesus Christ. A "What would Jesus have me do?" discernment framework offers a nuanced revival of the WWJD approach that moves beyond clichés to specific criteria. This prayerful, questioning practice provides an invitation to engage in deep discernment, enabling the truth of Christ to guide every decision, conversation, and action.

To help answer this question, we can develop a framework based on five crucial questions.

First, does our action align with the Great Commandment to love God and love our neighbor?[21] If it doesn't, it isn't worthy of our allegiance.

Second, does it exhibit the fruit of the Spirit (love, joy, peace, patience, kindness, goodness, faithfulness, gentleness, and self-control), or does it indulge the works of the flesh, such as anger or division?[22]

Third, does the decision seek God's kingdom first, or does it reflect self-interest and fear?

Fourth, could our actions harm our witness for Christ in the world?

Finally, have we prayed, searched the full Scriptures, and sought godly counsel about this issue and our response?

This framework, simple as it may be, requires intentional reflection and spiritual honesty, challenging us to make decisions not just in times of crisis but in the small, daily choices that shape our lives. By walking through these questions (which can be printed in checklist or diagram form), believers gain a litmus test for choices such as whom to vote for, how to respond to a contentious social issue, or whether to speak out against injustice. For example, if a social media post I draft fails the love and peace tests, perhaps I shouldn't post it.

Asking "What would Jesus have me do?" is another way of confessing Christ as Lord. Such questions are a practical form of virtue ethics, forming habits of Christlike decision-making.[23] This discernment practice reminds us that being citizens of God's kingdom means putting aside the pursuit of

21. Matt 22:37–40.

22. Gal 5:22–23.

23. Murphy et al., *Virtues and Practices.*

worldly power and embracing instead the transformative power of love, truth, and mercy.

ACCOUNTABILITY AND DISCIPLINE IN PUBLIC WITNESS

Discerning the right path isn't a journey we must take alone. As a body of believers, the Spirit of Jesus Christ calls us to be a community of accountability, where we watch over one another and hold each other accountable for the way we represent Christ in the world.

In an era where the lines between faith and political ideology have become blurred, the church must serve as a moral compass for its members, guiding them back to the truth when they stray from it. This requires courage, especially when confronting public sins that threaten to tarnish the church's witness.

Churches can take practical steps by forming accountability groups, where Christians involved in politics or public service come together to ensure their actions align with biblical ethics. The New Testament provides a model for this in Matt 18:15–17, where the church disciplines members who stray from the path of righteousness, not to punish, but to restore them.

Historically, churches have taken drastic steps to guard the purity of their witness, such as the Quakers disowning members who supported slavery.[24] While such actions may seem bold, they serve a critical role in upholding the integrity of the gospel.

Today, the church must be willing to call out actions that support nationalism, racism, or any ideology that undermines the gospel message, the righteousness and justice of God, the holiness and inclusivity of the Spirit, and the love and sacrifice of Christ. This discipline isn't about punishing or excluding but about protecting the church from the idols of the age and ultimately drawing its members back into the fullness of Christ's love.[25]

In doing so, the church offers an alternative to the toxic political ideologies that surround us, standing as a faithful witness to the kingdom of God where divine justice, radical love, abundant peace, and Spirit-empowered reconciliation reign. God's people must be countercultural. Kingdom citizenship sometimes requires the church to correct or even cut ties with

24. Hamm, *Quakers in America.*

25. Mouw, *Uncommon Decency.*

attitudes baptized by nationalist culture. Our allegiance to Christ must be visibly above all national or political allegiances.

May we not grow weary or bow to the siren songs of empire but rise as pilgrims who dare to speak truth, pursue justice, and carry the radiant scandal of the cross into every corner of public life until Christ's reign breaks forth in fullness, redemption, and glory.

7.

The Cross and the Flag

MANY PEOPLE TODAY ARE quick to bow before the idols of nation and tribe. Yet, Jesus Christ calls us to be a pilgrim people who move profoundly into a divine, holy, radical love that dismantles walls and heals ancient wounds. Here, on sacred ground, we listen for the voice of Christ inviting us beyond every boundary we've drawn into the wide embrace of God's reconciling grace.

THE CROSS ABOVE ALL

At the heart of Christian discipleship lies the way of the cross, the symbol of divine love that stands in judgment over all earthly powers and aspirations. Paul's bold declaration to "boast in the cross" (Gal 6:14) is an invitation to reject the hollow glories of status, power, ideology, flag, nation, and self-exaltation. The cross, in its scandalous self-giving love, challenges our world's pursuit of force and domination.

In Mark 8:34, Jesus calls his followers to "take up their cross," an invitation to embrace suffering, relinquishment, sacrifice, and self-giving love rather than the false promises of worldly power. The way of Christ, which is the path of cruciform love, offers no allegiance to the idols of a nation or tribe, no compromise with the powers that seek salvation through force.

As Stanley Hauerwas writes, the cross stands as God's eternal "no" to the powers of this world, rejecting salvation through coercion or national pride.[1] The very image of Jesus before Pilate, declaring that his kingdom isn't of this world, reminds us that Christ rejected the temptation to political revolution, demonstrating that true power lies not in the sword but in sacrificial love, not in power but in vulnerability, not in force but in reconciliation, and not in violence but shalom.

The cross of Christ calls us to renounce all allegiances that seek to elevate ourselves or our nation at the expense of others. When civil religion becomes a false gospel, we must turn to the cross as the true standard of the Christian life, a life marked by sacrificial love, laying down our lives for others.

JESUS IS LORD

Cross-centered allegiance isn't enough; we must follow allegiance up with convictions, actions, and a way of being. The confession that "Jesus is Lord" holds profound political implications.

In the first century, calling Jesus "Lord" was a bold declaration that Caesar was not. This pronouncement was an act of resistance against imperial idolatry, which demanded absolute loyalty to the emperor and posed a dangerous disruption and challenge to the prevailing principalities, rulers, ideologies, religions, institutions, and powers. We're sometimes tempted to forget how radical, wild, dangerous, costly, and risky such a declaration was for the early Christians and also for many Christians today across the world. For early Christians, declaring Jesus Christ to be Lord wasn't simply a spiritual statement but a radical political act that redefined loyalty and allegiance.

The affirmation of Christ's lordship above all earthly rulers undermines the claim of any political system or ideology that seeks to replace him. As we see in the Barmen Declaration of 1934, drafted by German theologians in response to Nazi ideology, "Jesus Christ . . . is the one Word of God whom we must trust and obey in life and death," rejecting any Führer or ideology that demands total allegiance.[2]

I'm writing this in 2025, the seventeen hundredth anniversary of the Nicene Creed, a bold and prophetic declaration that has stood the test of time as the church's explicit affirmation of Christ's lordship. Formulated in

1. Hauerwas and Willimon, *Resident Aliens*, 72. My words are a distilling of Hauerwas's thoughts, not a direct quote.

2. *Barmen Theological Declaration*, Thesis 1, 388.

AD 325, it unambiguously proclaims Jesus as "the only Son of God, eternally begotten of the Father," asserting his divinity and authority in the face of competing ideologies and claims.[3] In a world rife with power struggles and false claims to ultimate authority, the Nicene Creed remains a steadfast reminder that Jesus alone is Lord. This declaration calls on Christians to resist all other forms of idolatry (whether political, national, religious, racial, ethnic, ideological, or cultural) and to align their lives with the radical, transformative reign of Christ. His kingdom is defined by sacrificial love, divine righteousness, holy justice, unshakable joy, steadfast faith, astonishing compassion, countercultural reconciliation, and eternal hope.

This powerful declaration that Christ is Lord echoes throughout Christian history, reminding us that our ultimate loyalty must always lie with Christ alone. While love for country is permissible, it must never eclipse our devotion to Christ. When national symbols and political slogans become sacrosanct in our hearts, we risk falling into the sin of idolatry.

Our citizenship is in heaven. This truth relativizes any earthly citizenship, ensuring that all other allegiances remain subordinate to our identity in Christ. You and I must root our resistance to Christian nationalism, political populism, and cultural idolatries in the firm conviction that Christ is the sole Lord of our lives. This allegiance to Christ alone forms the bedrock of our Christian witness, challenging all other loyalties and reminding us of the call to follow the way of the cross.

PROPHETS VS. EMPIRES

The prophetic voices of the Bible are strikingly relevant in today's political climate. Their wise and courageous voices and themes offer us insights into God's heart and how empires can be confronted and subverted. The biblical prophets offer timeless wisdom for discerning the tension between God's kingdom and the allure of empire, power, and compromise.

The prophet Isaiah, for example, boldly confronted the pride of nations, denouncing their systemic injustices and abuse of the most vulnerable in society, especially when religious, social, and national rulers and institutions displaced God's law with worldly power.[4] His words against Assyria in Isa 10 exemplify the kind of prophetic resistance that critiques

3. "Nicene Creed," 58–59.

4. Brueggemann, *Isaiah 1–39*, on Isaiah's critique of Assyria and systemic injustice.

political oppression, calling the people of God to turn from false allegiances to Yahweh, their true Lord and King.

Similarly, Amos, whose words were as much an indictment of Israel as they were of the surrounding nations, denounced any form of nationalism that justified injustice. Amos didn't flinch in his refusal to say "my country, right or wrong," but instead called for humility, mercy, justice, righteousness, and repentance.[5]

Central to this biblical tradition is the example of Jesus, who embodied the ultimate rejection of political messianism.[6] When the people attempted to crown him as king by force, he withdrew to a quiet place (John 6:15). When his disciples sought to restore the kingdom to Israel, he redirected their gaze beyond nationalism to the global mission of God's kingdom (Acts 1:6–8). Jesus's refusal to endorse the Zealot revolt against Rome or to partake in ethnic hatred (by including both a tax collector and a Zealot among his apostles) highlights the radical alternative he embodied.[7] His kingdom was one of grace, not violence, of reconciliation, not division.

This prophetic challenge to empires and their agendas, abuses, violence, institutions, and rulers resounds throughout the biblical prophets and the words and actions of Jesus Christ. What is the lesson for us? Such prophetic language and deeds underscore the biblical call to resist conflating the kingdom of God with any earthly empire or nation. Discernment amid populist deception isn't new, as God's people have always needed to distinguish God's voice from nationalistic propaganda. The church, when faithful, remains a moral and spiritual witness, lifting the cross above any flag.

CONFESSING CHRIST, NOT COUNTRY

The Barmen Declaration of 1934 stands as a bold and prophetic witness against the fusion of nationalism and faith during the rise of Nazi Germany. As I previously explored in this book, it's striking that, amid the horrific rise of Hitler's ideology, a group of Christian leaders led by Karl Barth penned this declaration to reaffirm that the church's sole allegiance is to Jesus Christ. Barmen's first thesis boldly declared, "Jesus Christ is the one Word of God,"

5. Jeremias, *Book of Amos*, on Amos's condemnation of nationalistic idolatry.

6. Wright, *Jesus and the Victory of God*, on Jesus rejecting political messianism and nationalist hopes.

7. Hauerwas and Willimon, *Resident Aliens*.

rejecting the idolatrous claims of the Nazi regime that sought to distort the Christian faith.[8] This wasn't merely theological rhetoric but a daring political stand: to refuse the national ideology of Hitler's "Aryan Christianity" and to proclaim that no political leader, no earthly power, politics, or ideology, could command the conscience of followers of Jesus Christ.

The cost of this faithfulness was immense. Pastors like Martin Niemöller, who dared to stand firm against the Nazi misuse of the church, were imprisoned. Many Christians were killed standing up for their conviction that Jesus Christ is the one Word of God and no Führer, no national ideology, no political agenda or party could bind Christian conscience. Their willingness to bear the cross cost them everything.

This spirit of resistance continued in the Belhar Confession of 1986, which emerged during the apartheid era in South Africa.[9] Like Barmen, Belhar proclaimed the unity of the church in Christ, rejecting the apartheid state's theological distortion that sought to separate believers along racial lines. Both confessions demonstrated an unwavering commitment to the gospel, set against the idolatries of nationalism. We need more examples of such courage and prophetic speech and action today, wherever political, state, and ideological violence and domination threaten humanity and the core commitment to Christ and his lordship, gospel, and kingdom.

In recent times, Eastern Orthodox leaders have also spoken out against the fusion of church and state, condemning the misuse of faith to justify war and political power.[10] These confessions stand as a collective, historical voice reminding the church of the biblical calling to resist populist, partisan, and political idolatry and declare allegiance to Christ alone.

As the church has done in times of crisis, so must we today. We must confess Christ and his kingdom, not country, as our ultimate loyalty. This refusal to bow to political idols echoes across history, urging those who are faithful to Jesus Christ to take a stand against the dangerous conflation of faith and nationalism.

8. Evangelische Kirche in Deutschland, *Barmer Theologische Erklärung*.

9. *Belhar Confession* (1986).

10. Interparliamentary Assembly on Orthodoxy, "Statement on the Invasion in Ukraine."

LISTENING TO THE GLOBAL CHURCH

The echo chamber of nationalism often drowns out the voices of the marginalized. In this environment, we must learn to listen deeply, especially to the voices of the global church. For many Western Christians, especially in Western Europe and North America, our perspective is often limited by the bubble of cultural privilege. Yet, in the words of Lamin Sanneh, "World Christianity" is a vital check against provincialism.[11] It's the global body of Christ that offers insights from contexts shaped by violence, persecution, and marginalization. It's in these spaces that we find wisdom and prophetic clarity, offering us lessons in resisting the seduction of political power.

Take, for example, the testimony of Rwandan church leaders in the aftermath of the 1994 genocide.[12] Their grief-stricken witness warns against the dangers of ethnic nationalism, even among Christians, and urges the church never to baptize tribalism. In the Middle East, Christians who have suffered under both Islamist and nationalist regimes caution us about the perils of fusing faith with political power.

By hearing their stories of complicity and resistance, we sharpen our ability to discern the dangers within our context. We must resist the temptation to idolize our political systems since the kingdom of God is multinational (Rev 7:9). We must learn to be "quick to listen, slow to speak" (Jas 1:19), humbly acknowledging that our brothers and sisters from around the world may see truths that we, in our cultural captivity, may miss. Through this humility, we step outside our blind spots, guarding ourselves against the complacency that comes with majority status.

When I interviewed Lamin Sanneh in April 2015, he said the following to me.

> We in the West are a confident and articulate people, and theology has served us well as a vehicle of our aspirations, desires, and goals. There is no shortage of theological books on all sorts of imaginable subjects, with how-to-do manuals instructing us about effective ministry, how to fix our emotions, how to affirm our individual identity and promote our choices and preferences, how to change society through political action, how to raise funds and build bigger churches, about investing in strategic coalitions, etc. All this language leaves us little time or space to listen to God with the chance that God may have something, and even something else,

11. Sanneh, *Whose Religion Is Christianity*, 22–25.

12. Longman, *Christianity and Genocide in Rwanda*, 1–5.

> to say to us, especially if that something else challenges what we want to hear. On the matter of the cultural captivity of the gospel in the West, the renewal of World Christianity may have lessons to teach us all.[13]

May we have hearts and minds open to listening and learning from the global church.

A HUMBLE HEART AND WILLINGNESS TO REPENT

The challenge of listening globally is inextricably linked to a call for humility, both personal and communal. We need humility to recognize and be open to changing our ignorance, hardness of heart, distorted perspectives, or myopia. Even the most sincere Christians can be unknowingly captive to cultural and nationalist biases, as the story of Peter in Acts 10 forcefully illustrates. Peter, a loyal apostle, had his cultural prejudices overturned by a divine revelation, showing us that discernment involves openness to correction. If Peter could be unaware of his biases, how much more must we remain vigilant against the seductions of nationalism and political idolatry?

We need the Holy Spirit to give us a spiritual posture that embraces humility and repentance. Just as Peter's transformation led to a new understanding of God's will, so must we allow Christ's Spirit to lead us to deeper self-awareness. Churches can create spaces where the community collectively confesses corporate sins, including past or current racism, nationalism, and injustices the church is complicit in.[14] We have an opportunity to model a posture of continuous reformation. By admitting our failings, we break free from the political idols that claim our loyalty. Repentance isn't just an intellectual task but a spiritual one, and not just a personal act but a communal one. Repentance is rooted in the heart, enabling us to turn from pride and idolatry.

The emphasis on repentance reminds us that breaking the spell of nationalism isn't about winning intellectual debates but about cultivating a Christlike character. Humility (which is the opposite of nationalism's arrogance) becomes the antidote to idolatry. Service (which is the opposite of the grasping and controlling nature of political idolatry) is God's character made manifest among us and in our witness to the world. Love (which is

13. Hill, "Conversation with Lamin Sanneh."

14. Tutu, *No Future Without Forgiveness.*

the opposite of the divisions and violence of many forms of populism) is the way we show the world we are Jesus Christ's disciples.

This ongoing work of repentance and self-examination isn't just about acknowledging past mistakes but seeking true freedom in the transforming power of the gospel. By living out these practices, we embody the vision of a church continually being reformed, a living testimony of grace and humility that transcends the political idolatry of our time.

STEEPED IN SCRIPTURE, PRAYER, AND COMMUNITY

We're drowning in online distractions and noise. Every screen is saturated with half-truths, ideological performances, political spin, and biased narratives. Christ's call for his disciples to be discerning has never been more urgent. The remedy for the spiritual fog of misinformation and disinformation lies in grounding ourselves daily in the Bible, prayer, and local, reflective, countercultural, discerning Christian communities.

Just as sheep know the voice of their Shepherd (John 10:4), Christians must attune their hearts to the clarity of Scripture to counter the static of political ideologies. To do this, a daily regimen of Scripture reading, especially the Gospels and prophets, alongside current events, provides a sacred filter through which we process the chaos of the world. As we read, the Spirit of Christ reminds us that our allegiance is to Jesus, to his Way, and to God's kingdom, and not to the fleeting kingdoms of this world.

Equally important is prayer. James 1:5 invites us to ask for wisdom liberally and without reproach. Before reacting to a political headline or casting a vote, prayer is an act of surrender: "Lord, guide me." By confessing our biases to God, we allow divine truth to shape our hearts and actions, leading us out of the grip of ideology and into the freedom of the Spirit.

But this individual practice must never be divorced from the community that Christ calls us into. The church is meant to be a living, breathing counterculture to the world's noise, a place where truth is spoken in love, where discernment is sharpened in fellowship, and where the Spirit's wisdom flows through the shared life of God's people. As the world becomes increasingly divided, isolated, and fragmented, Christians must gather not just for corporate worship but also for ongoing dialogue about the pressing issues of the day. In these spaces, the Spirit invites us to wrestle with the realities of our time, asking not just, "What's true?" but also, "What's God calling us to do in response?" A discerning community listens to each other, prays together, and holds each other accountable to the way of the cross. By committing to communal discernment, we strengthen each other's resolve, learn to hear God's voice more clearly and become a prophetic witness to the world. We choose to be a people deeply rooted in Scripture, united in prayer, and shaped by a love that transcends all earthly divides. Through this, the church becomes a lighthouse of hope, not only in a fragmented world but for a generation desperate to hear the voice of truth amid the chaos.

Such practices aren't merely disciplines but spiritual warfare. They form our very lives with the "belt of truth" and "sword of the Spirit" (Eph 6:14, 17). When we live in constant prayer, Scripture, and discerning faith communities, we align our hearts with God's peace, ready to resist the noise of fear, anxiety, division, animosity, and falsehood with confidence, hope, shalom, love, and clarity.

COMMUNAL DISCERNMENT AND DIALOGUE

I'll keep emphasizing the communal dimension to our discipleship and resistance to all forms of spiritual compromise and idolatry until I'm blue in the face. Just as individual discernment requires rootedness in prayer and Scripture, so too does the church, as the body of Christ, need communal practices of shared wisdom.

The early church offers us the model: in Acts 15, when facing contentious issues, they gathered, prayed, and allowed the Holy Spirit to guide them together. This communal discernment serves as a corrective against the polarization we face today. Churches can form "kingdom discernment groups," spaces where believers pray, discuss, and listen for the Spirit's leading in the midst of current issues.

When we bring current events to the table, seasoned with Scripture and prayer, we create a dynamic that goes beyond politics and partisanship. In these spaces, we can practice dialogical prayer, where differing opinions aren't only heard but lifted up in prayer for wisdom, compassion, discernment, and unity. The church becomes a community not of division, but of healing, where even conflicting views can be held in the light of Christ's love. By engaging in corporate confession (repenting for ways we've allowed nationalism or partisanship to overshadow the cross) we find ourselves returning to the center of Christ's gospel.

These communal practices, rooted in Scripture and prayer, build habits of clarity, humility, and courage. They remind us that, as the body of Christ, we're to discern and act together, not in isolation. The church, as the "pillar and bulwark of truth" (1 Tim 3:15), stands firm against the deceptions of our time, embodying a kingdom that transcends the divisions of the world.

In the Micah Global book I edited called *Relentless Love*, I wrote,

> The gospel should never be reduced to a privatized, individualistic gospel that is only about God dealing with personal sin and pain. God redeems us from the power of sin and death. Through Jesus's death and resurrection, our personal sins are forgiven, and we are set free *from* sin and death *to* a new life of fullness, hope, faith, love, and glory. But the full gospel of Jesus is much more expansive and cosmic than mere personal or individual forgiveness of sin. The gospel story extends from creation to new creation, from Genesis to Revelation. The gospel tells us that in Jesus Christ, God restores all things, all people, and all creation to God's originally intended shalom: God's perfection, glory, justice, harmony, peace, flourishing, goodness, and wholeness. The world is tired of false and inadequate forms of the gospel. Christians are, too. When people hear a gospel that is about personal forgiveness and salvation *and* also about God forming a people who join with Jesus Christ in restoring all creation to God's perfect justice, peace, love, and freedom, they hear the gospel as good news.[15]

We must cultivate communal practices of discernment, contemplation, dialogue, and action if we are going to challenge the political and other idolatries of our age and offer the living Way of Jesus Christ.

DEFENDING TRUTH IN AN AGE OF LIES

Our age is awash with misinformation and disinformation. God's call to uphold truth has never been more pressing. Christian nationalism, populist movements, and ideological fervor thrive on spreading false narratives that distort reality for political gain.

As followers of Jesus Christ, he calls us to stand for truth, even when we're tempted to absorb lies, even when dedication to the truth is costly and dangerous, and even when it's unpopular or uncomfortable. Our first step in this discernment process is to question the sources of information

15. Hill, *Relentless Love*, 10–11.

we consume rigorously. Do we rely on social media echo chambers, or do we seek out reputable sources? What biases and ideologies shape the discourse in our preferred traditional or new media spaces? Are we discerning enough to recognize the bias in the narratives we encounter, and do we challenge ourselves to look beyond surface-level arguments?

Truth-telling isn't a passive act, but a spiritual discipline. Telling the truth in love isn't a posture of timidity or wishy-washy, insipid responses to untruths. An example is how some Christians had to publicly debunk the QAnon conspiracy within their churches as an act of faithfulness. Ephesians 6:14 speaks of the "belt of truth" that holds everything together in the spiritual armor of God. By committing ourselves to truth, we resist the pull of ideological propaganda and the forces that seek to manipulate our beliefs. Ideas are often weaponized in our society, so we must find ways to communicate truth with clarity and confidence, but also with grace, humility, and love.

As Christians, we must take responsibility for the words we share. "You shall not give false testimony" (Exod 20:16) isn't a command meant to be ignored in the age of fake news. And yet, truth-telling often requires more than just a passive defense of facts; it asks for courage and humility. Truth-telling requires us to speak out gently yet firmly when we encounter conspiracy theories, bigotry, or falsehoods from others, even when it comes at the cost of relationships or social capital. Defending truth means actively pursuing wisdom and standing firm in the reality of God's word, regardless of the cultural or political pressures around us.

PROPHETIC COURAGE IN PUBLIC

Once we have discerned the truth, the next step is to live it out boldly, even when it requires us to make a sacrifice. The biblical prophets weren't only truth-tellers; they were also brave enough to act on God's commands, even at the risk of persecution. In Acts 5:29, when the apostles were ordered to remain silent, they declared, "We must obey God rather than people." This isn't just a call to intellectual discernment but a call to courageous action in the face of injustice, oppression, and lies. In our context, this might mean standing up against the idolatries of nationalism, racial injustice, violence against undocumented immigrants, exploitation of working-class people struggling with the impact of globalization, or the glorification of power that diminishes the humanity of others.

In the book I edited for Micah Global, I quoted Orlando Costas, saying,

> When the church ignores issues of justice, peacemaking, poverty, and reconciliation, it denies the call of God and refuses to reflect the image of Christ. We can never allow our gospel to become so compromised and disfigured that it becomes about "a conscience-soothing Jesus, with an unscandalous cross, an other-worldly kingdom, a private, inwardly limited spirit, a pocket God, a spiritualized Bible, and an escapist church [whose] goal is a happy, comfortable, and successful life, obtainable through the forgiveness of an abstract sinfulness by faith in an unhistorical Christ."[16]

Prophetic courage calls us to ask the hard questions: How does my faith challenge the political ideologies I encounter? How can I remain faithful to Christ when the world around me demands conformity? Jesus warned us that his Way wouldn't always be easy, but he also promised that in standing firm, we would find true life. Remember, the early martyrs didn't simply resist the powers that be; they boldly proclaimed, "Jesus is Lord," a declaration that threatened the very foundations of the empire.[17] Today, we must be prepared to speak the same truth, whether it is to confront the political powers that abuse their authority or to challenge ideologies that seek to divide and conquer.

In our discipleship to Jesus Christ, let's show that prophetic courage isn't fueled by pride, but by humility. It's rooted in the love of Christ, the willingness to serve, and the desire to be faithful witnesses to a kingdom that transcends earthly power. When we're confronted with the pressures of the world, let's stand tall and boldly proclaim the gospel, even in the face of criticism, suffering, or rejection. This is the cost of discipleship, and it's the path that Christ calls us to walk. Our Creator and our Messiah invite us to be not just critics of nationalism, but bold and Christlike witnesses in the public arena, echoing Paul's statement, "I am not ashamed of the gospel," even when the gospel stands against the nationalistic tide.[18]

May we rest here a moment, hearts open to the Spirit who breaks dividing walls. Let's not make peace with the divisions we've built and, instead, may the Spirit trouble our comfort until every barrier falls before the reconciling power of Jesus Christ.

16. Costas, *Christ Outside the Gate*, 80; Hill, *Relentless Love*, 9.

17. Gorman, *Cruciformity*.

18. Rom 1:16.

8.

Jesus Is Lord

When the noise of empires fades and the dust of rulers, principalities, and powers settle, what remains is God's summons to follow Jesus Christ and his everlasting rule and reign. At this moment, regardless of our culture, era, or context, God calls us to walk the humble road of Christ, carrying not banners of power but the cross of a love that dares to redeem all things.

ONE KING, ONE KINGDOM

The church, at its core, is a declaration: an assertion that Jesus Christ is Lord and King, and that his kingship and kingdom are eternal, reigning supreme over all powers, principalities, lords, rulers, and empires. In the words of Jesus, "They're not of the world, just as I'm not of the world" (John 17:16). This statement encapsulates the identity of the church and all those who call themselves followers of Jesus Christ. We are a people under the lordship of Christ, and this allegiance shapes everything about who we are and how we live. Our lives are marked by a higher calling, a kingdom not of this world, but of heaven. It's a kingdom that stands in contrast to the world's empires: whether political, national, or ideological.

Jesus, the true King of kings, calls us to live not by the status quo of the world, but by the radical values of his kingdom. Disciples of Jesus, as citizens of his kingdom and pilgrims on the way to our complete union with him in his glory, must choose to be salt and light (Matt 5:13–16), shining in the darkness, offering an alternative society that rejects the allure of power, pride, violence, and division.

The Spirit of Christ fills the church, empowering us to embody the new creation that God has promised. As people of the Jesus Way, submitting to the lordship of Christ, and declaring his rule and reign, we're a community that operates under a different rule: one of justice, righteousness, grace, kindness, forgiveness, hope, humility, mercy, and love.

To say "Jesus is Lord" isn't a neutral statement; it's a proclamation that every earthly allegiance must bow to the supremacy of Christ.[1] And because Christ's reign is eternal, transcendent, and countercultural, we followers of Christ must sometimes find ourselves out of step with the culture, rejecting nationalism, tribalism, political allegiances, the gods of empires and nations, and other earthly idols.

By boldly declaring Jesus as Lord, the church embraces its calling to challenge any power that seeks to distort God's truth. The Christian faith calls us to stand apart from worldly ideologies, living not according to human laws of status and power, but according to the divine law of love, truth, righteousness, peace, and justice. God has given us a high calling to imitate and conform to Jesus Christ, as followers of his Way, and as citizens of God's eternal kingdom.

ALLEGIANCE BEYOND BORDERS AND TRANSCENDING TRIBALISM

If Jesus is truly Lord, then no earthly boundary, no tribal affiliation, no political partisanship, no ideological agenda, no culture war, and no commitments that seek to transcend his lordship can define who we are. Our primary identity is found in Christ, and it transcends all ethnic, national, political, racial, gender, class, and social divisions. In Gal 3:28, Paul boldly declares, "There is neither Jew nor Greek, slave nor free, male nor female, for you are all one in Christ Jesus." This radical reordering of human identity is the foundation of the church's global mission.

As Christians, our allegiance is to a kingdom that has no borders, no nationalism, and no racism. We are part of a "third race," as the early church described itself, a new people united not by geography but by the Spirit.[2] These new people (a new creation in Christ) effectively create a new supra-national identity (as hinted in the *Epistle to Diognetus*, where every

1. Gorman, *Cruciformity*.
2. Tertullian, *Apology*, 45–47.

foreign land was like a homeland and vice versa).[3] The church, as Stanley Hauerwas and William H. Willimon observe, is the only true global political entity, transcending the confines of nations, cultures, and ideologies, whereas the nation-state is inherently tribal.[4] The church is universal and eternal (transformed and raised to life in Christ), whereas nation states are particular and passing away. Our faith isn't tied to our nationality; our primary identity is as new people united in Christ and redeemed by his death and resurrection. We are pilgrims on the way to our heavenly home and citizenship in God's glorious, matchless, eternal kingdom.

This vision of the church as a new humanity, gathered from "every tribe and tongue" (Rev 7:9), challenges the very notion of Christian nationalism. How can we be nationalists when our brothers and sisters in Christ are citizens of nations we might regard as "other" or even adversarial? This theological framework calls Christians to prioritize their loyalty to Christ above all other loyalties and to view their fellow believers as family, regardless of geographical boundaries. It's this new humanity, united under Christ, that offers the world an alternative to the division and enmity of earthly kingdoms. The church's unity in Christ is a powerful testimony that the reign of Christ is a kingdom without boundaries.

Our reflections on allegiance beyond borders and divisions, and the Spirit's empowerment to transcend all tribalism, set a tone of celebration: the church is the family of God, in which worldly enmities are overcome by Christ (Eph 2:14). This conviction serves as the antidote to the exclusionary mindset of Christian nationalism. It's hard to be a nationalist when you realize fellow citizens of Jesus's kingdom come from nations your earthly country might consider "other" or even an enemy. Jesus's lordship creates a new humanity, and our loyalty to him relativizes all other loyalties.

RADICAL INCLUSION IN THE EARLY CHURCH

In the first centuries of the church, Christianity's radical inclusivity stood as a prophetic act against the deeply entrenched hierarchies of the Roman Empire. Jesus's lordship didn't simply demand devotion in private; it reshaped social realities. The early Christian community, particularly in its house churches, was one of profound reversal, where those who were treated harshly in the world (enslaved people, women, some minority ethnic

3. *Epistle to Diognetus* 5.1–5.5, in *Apostolic Fathers*.

4. Hauerwas and Willimon, *Resident Aliens*, 90–92.

groups, those struggling with illnesses and poverty, and the marginalized) became equally beloved and honored in Christ. The Lord's Supper wasn't just a ritual but an invitation to radical equality, honor, human dignity, and inclusion. Jews and gentiles, once separated by centuries of animosity, now sat side by side as brothers and sisters, a direct embodiment of the gospel's power to break down dividing walls (Eph 2:14).

The *Epistle to Diognetus* captures this ethos well: "They love all men [*sic*], and by all men are persecuted . . . . They are in the flesh, but do not live after the flesh . . . . Every foreign land is to them as their native country."[5] This passage reveals the early church's revolutionary stance: its members refused to be defined by the tribal, national, or political boundaries of the Roman Empire. Instead, their identity was rooted in the reign of Christ, which transcended race, class, and ethnicity. Through this radical inclusion, the early Christians embodied a kingdom that stood in stark contrast to the empire's oppressive structure.

Their unity wasn't only a theological declaration but a social one that defied Roman imperialism and nationalism by making space for all, especially the most marginalized. As such, their example offers a blueprint for today's churches, showing that to declare "Jesus is Lord" is to live out a kingdom that defies earthly polarizations, politicizations, divisions, and structures. These early Christians navigated their social and political worlds by adhering to Jesus's lordship, and the world took notice. Their unity across cultural and ethnic lines became a compelling testimony to the watching world (John 17:21). This, too, is a call for followers of Jesus to become a "contrast society," standing against the idols of nationalism, racism, and division. Returning to the spirituality of Jesus has always been the answer to the empire's pressures.

SOLIDARITY ACROSS BORDERS

The spirit of unity and radical discipleship lived out by the early church found its echoes in later periods of history, especially in the abolition of slavery and the resistance against apartheid. The global Christian networks of the eighteenth and nineteenth centuries, committed to ending the transatlantic slave trade, are potent examples of how "Jesus is Lord" became a rallying cry for justice that transcended national borders. Christians in Britain, like William Wilberforce, corresponded with and partnered with

5. *Epistle to Diognetus* 5.1–5.5, in *Apostolic Fathers*.

fellow Christians in the United States and elsewhere, driven by their shared conviction that the gospel demanded the dignity and freedom of every human being.[6] They stood in defiance of national interests and systemic oppression, bound not by the ideologies and prejudices of the day, but by a common allegiance to Christ Jesus.

Similarly, during South Africa's apartheid regime, Christians around the world joined forces to support the Confessing Churches in South Africa, whose stance against the racial injustice of apartheid resulted in the powerful Belhar Confession.[7] In this moment, the global church once again demonstrated the power of unity in Christ over nationalism, recognizing that racism isn't only a political evil but a heresy that contradicts the gospel itself. The World Council of Churches provided material support to anti-apartheid efforts, reinforcing that walls, boundaries, borders, races, politics, nations, or political systems can't confine the kingdom of God.[8]

Even under communism, Christians from various countries built solidarity networks to resist the state-sponsored atheism of the East. These underground movements (often crossing the Iron Curtain through letters, prayers, clandestine meetings, and other forms of support), embodied Christ's lordship in a way that transcended national allegiances. This example reinforces the church's vocation as a transnational, global body. We are a God-glorifying, Christ-following, and Spirit-formed and -empowered body that doesn't merely focus on its own nation's welfare but reaches out in compassion, mercy, and solidarity to the suffering of all. This stands in direct opposition to nationalism and the politics of exclusion.

These global Christian solidarity movements emphasize that Jesus's lordship calls us to a transcendent, kingdom-driven unity that transcends all boundaries. It challenges us as followers of Christ today to look beyond national, political, or partisan lines and ask, "How are we living out our allegiance to Christ in a divided world?" The examples of abolition, apartheid resistance, and underground networks remind us that Jesus calls us to stand for justice and reconciliation, no matter the cost. These stories invite us to be the church that crosses borders, speaking with one voice against the powers that oppress and divide.

Christ's body is intercultural and transnational. Christian activism and witness demonstrate this reality. We must emphasize the catholicity

6. Belmonte, *William Wilberforce*.

7. *Belhar Confession* (online).

8. De Gruchy, *Church Struggle in South Africa*, 165–70.

(universality) of the church, which is an idea dear to many theologians (e.g., Lesslie Newbigin's vision of a worldwide church bearing one witness).[9] Thankfully, the historical and global church offers many concrete heroes and heroines to emulate, demonstrating that declaring "Jesus is Lord" often involved networking across empires to embody kingdom values. These ordinary, faithful Christians chose the Way of Christ over the way of nationalism and political idolatry, and acted with costly and dangerous courage. We can do the same.

SERVANT LEADERSHIP, NOT DOMINATION

At the heart of the gospel is a call to a leadership that looks nothing like the world's. In a world where power often equates to control, authority can be wielded as domination, and influence is frequently associated with status. However, Jesus offers us a radically different model of leadership: the servant leader.[10] The very kingship of Christ isn't about coercion but about sacrifice.

When we declare "Jesus is Lord," we're pledging allegiance to a kingdom whose currency is humility, grace, and self-giving love. As Jesus showed by washing his disciples' feet (John 13), our leadership must be defined not by grandeur but by service, not by control but by care.

The church, as the body of Christ, is called to be a contrast community in a world dominated by power struggles.[11] A church that reflects the lordship of Christ must model leadership that is humble, accountable, and primarily concerned with the well-being of others. This means that any form of leadership in the church that mirrors the hierarchical, authoritarian structures of the world (be it celebrity pastors or power-hungry political alliances) must be rejected.

Instead, we celebrate servant leadership, where the true measure of success is the depth of love and service, not the number of followers or political influence. By embracing this model, the church becomes a living witness to a kingdom that operates in direct opposition to the world's ideologies of power.

Leaders within the church must continually ask: "Am I leading in a way that reflects Jesus's example? Am I pointing to Christ's lordship through

9. Newbigin, *Household of God*, 121–23.

10. Greenleaf, *Servant Leadership*; Stott, *Basic Christian Leadership*.

11. Hauerwas and Willimon, *Resident Aliens*.

my service, my humility, my care?" For the body of believers, this means recognizing that authentic leadership is not about influence or control, but about laying down one's life for others.

ECONOMICS OF THE KINGDOM

The implications of declaring "Jesus is Lord" stretch beyond our personal lives into the economic systems we support. If Christ is truly Lord, then we must radically transform our approach to money and possessions.

The early church, as described in Acts 2:44–45, lived out a model of communal sharing where no one was in need, a striking contrast to the individualistic, profit-driven systems of the world. The kingdom of God operates on the economy of grace, where wealth isn't hoarded but shared, not worshiped but stewarded for the common good.

Society often tells us that security comes from amassing wealth, that our worth is tied to what we own, and that those experiencing poverty or disadvantage are to be left to fend for themselves.

Let me offer three examples from the United States. First, while "America First" nationalism might encourage hoarding resources or cutting aid, the kingdom ethic encourages open-handedness and concern for economically disadvantaged communities overseas as "our own."

Similarly, while some political ideologies may overlook or even disparage working-class rural and regional communities, the kingdom ethic calls us to recognize their struggles as our own. Instead of dismissing or reinforcing their sense of abandonment (or throwing insults at them and calling them racist), the kingdom of God urges us to extend compassion, offer practical support, and listen to them with empathy as they share their pain (and, sometimes, trauma). Jesus calls us to open our hearts and hands, not just to economically disadvantaged communities overseas, but to those within our nation who feel left behind, ensuring that no one is forgotten or excluded in God's economy of care.

Finally, Christ's kingdom ethic calls us to welcome the stranger, especially undocumented migrants, as Christ would. Instead of seeing them as outsiders, we are called to offer hospitality, protection, and justice, recognizing that their dignity and worth are inseparable from our shared humanity. In Christ's kingdom, we're called to love our neighbors: not just those who look like us, but those who are far off, those who are often invisible in society.

This means that the church, as a contrast-community of believers and disciples, must prioritize economic justice, seeking to care for those experiencing poverty and exploitation, advocate for fair wages, stand up for working-class communities left behind by technologies and globalization, and advocate for immigrants who live in fear of deportation while struggling to feed their dependents. Let's lead lives that reflect our trust in God rather than in material wealth. Whether it's through supporting local initiatives, advocating for policy changes that lift the marginalized, or simply sharing resources within the community, the church must reject the idol of money and embrace a kingdom economy that values people over possessions.[12]

Just as Jesus taught us that we can't serve both God and money (Luke 16:13), so must we live in a way that declares our allegiance to Christ over the systems of greed and consumerism. Jesus calls us to be a community of generosity, to care for those experiencing poverty and vulnerability, and to stand for justice and equity in the broader world.

By living out these economic principles, the church provides a tangible witness to the world that true freedom and security are found not in wealth and power, but in Christ's lordship and our humble, loving, compassionate service. God's invitation to economic justice and shared life isn't merely an ideal; it is a practical, radical expression of Christ's kingdom that challenges the status quo and invites us into a life of sacrificial love and justice.

SUSTAINING HOPE AND PERSEVERANCE

Numerous challenges, obstacles, and temptations threaten to stop us from living under Christ's lordship in a world often at odds with his kingdom. Our need for personal perseverance and hope is critical, since compromise and despair threaten our faithfulness to Christ Jesus, our Lord.

Short-term satisfaction, external performances, instant results, inflated egotism, frenetic activity, and the perpetual noise of distraction drive our culture. So, the discipline of sustaining hope becomes a sacred task. We draw on the words of Heb 12:1–2, which urges followers of Jesus to "run with perseverance the race marked out for us, fixing our eyes on Jesus, the pioneer and perfecter of faith." The call isn't to merely survive but to flourish in faith amid opposition, to see through the fog of the world's

12. Wright, *Mission of God*, 303–8. Wright writes about the "economy of God's mission" that challenges human economic structures.

ideologies, to anchor our hearts in the eternal truths of the gospel, and to be a people of character, humility, love, inclusion, and service in societies that too often value performance, ego, ambition, exclusion, and grasping.

One of the ways we nurture perseverance is through daily practices of prayer, contemplation, and Scripture reading. When we pray "Your kingdom come" (Matt 6:10), we don't merely utter words; we speak with faith that this kingdom is coming, and it is breaking in now, even amid trials. The stories of the saints, persecuted believers, and martyrs offer us real-life examples of perseverance. By learning about their steadfastness, whether it's from early Christian martyrs or modern-day persecuted, suffering followers, we build our courage. The "cloud of witnesses" (Heb 12:1) offers a chorus of encouragement as we take our place in the story.

Cultivating gratitude in our daily lives also strengthens our hope. When we choose to see even the smallest signs of God's kingdom (whether it's a reconciling conversation, a moment of justice, or a life transformed by love), we build resilience. This practice of noticing and thanking God for the "small victories" helps to counteract the discouragement that so easily creeps in.

In this pilgrimage of hope, we turn our gaze to the ultimate fulfillment of God's promise: Christ's rule and reign, not only in the future but already in our hearts today. As we rest in this truth, we become increasingly equipped to persevere, not as victims of circumstance, but as victors in Christ, who has already won the ultimate victory on the cross. This hopeful perseverance isn't passive; it's an active engagement with the kingdom of God, even when the world offers nothing but opposition. We sustain our followership of Jesus (including our allegiance, activism, hope, and perseverance) by abiding in Christ (John 15:4–5). In nurturing this hope, we embrace spirituality and discipleship that acknowledge the struggle while firmly placing our trust in God's faithfulness.

WORSHIP AS POLITICAL WITNESS

Worship, at its heart, isn't merely a performance, production, or personal act but a communal declaration that Christ is Lord above all powers, ideologies, political idolatries, and nationalistic claims.[13] Every gathering of believers to sing, pray, and break bread is a counter-narrative to the empire's grasp.

13. Smith, *Desiring the Kingdom*.

By declaring Jesus as Lord, we make a statement (one that resounds across time and space) that no earthly ruler, no political system, no populist rhetoric, no illiberal or racist imagination, no progressive or liberal ideology, and no flag or nation holds ultimate authority.[14] This is why corporate worship is an essential act of resistance to the idolatry of nationalism. Each song we sing, each prayer we lift, each element of the Eucharist we partake in is a declaration of allegiance to Christ and his kingdom, not to any temporal power.

One powerful way to embody this resistance is by creating space in worship for prayers that transcend national borders. For example, praying regularly for other nations and their leaders, especially those that might be seen as "enemies" by our national government, is an act of profound countercultural witness. This kind of prayer reorients our hearts toward the global body of Christ, reminding us that our primary citizenship isn't in a nation-state, but in the kingdom of God.

Another way to embody resistance is through symbolic acts in our worship spaces. Some congregations, for example, have chosen to remove national flags from their sanctuaries to avoid confusing the kingdom of God with any one political entity.[15] Others might choose to display a variety of flags, representing the global church and our heart for all the nations of the earth, reminding everyone that the body of Christ transcends ethnic, political, national, and cultural boundaries.

The Eucharist (Communion or the Lord's Supper) itself is a radical political act.[16] In eating from one loaf and drinking from one cup, we declare that we are one people under the lordship of Christ, regardless of our earthly backgrounds. The Lord's Supper is a prophetic act looking forward to the great banquet of God's kingdom, where every tribe, nation, and tongue will be united in worship (Rev 7:9). Even in the words of the liturgy (whether it's the familiar declaration of "Christ has died, Christ is risen, Christ will come again" or other proclamations), we make a public statement about where history is headed. The gathered church, in worship, makes a declaration to the world that the kingdom of God is here and will come in fullness, and that no earthly power can eclipse or prevent it.

Communal and public witness through worship forms and shapes the congregation's identity. It trains our hearts to see Christ as the ultimate

14. Kreider, *Patient Ferment of the Early Church.*

15. Leeman, *How the Nations Rage.*

16. Wright, *Surprised by Hope.*

authority and all other allegiances as secondary. As we gather together, we remind one another that Jesus's lordship has profound implications not only for our private lives but for the world's powers and principalities. In this way, worship becomes more than a personal escape or emotional uplift; it becomes a political act of resistance, a public demonstration and proclamation of the supremacy of our King Jesus, and a declaration of the values of Christ's kingdom in a world that often chooses the way of empire. Through our worship, we practice the radical hospitality, inclusion, allegiance, peace, and unity that Jesus inaugurated.

DISCIPLING FOR PUBLIC LIFE

As the church continues to engage with the pressing issues of our time, it must rise to the challenge of discipling believers not just for personal morality or church roles but for their vocation as citizens of the kingdom of God. Discipleship can't remain confined to Sunday services and personal piety. Our discipleship to Jesus Christ must encompass the world in which we live daily. The practice of faith must be integrated into our civic lives, guiding how we interact with the world around us.

Churches can be proactive in offering classes, workshops, and small groups that bridge the gap between Sunday worship and Monday reality. For example, hosting forums that discuss faithful political engagement, without endorsing any political party, can help Christians understand how biblical ethics shape their civic responsibilities. Such forums can explore Catholic Social Teaching, Protestant political thought, themes in public theology and ethics, and the broader biblical mandate to seek the welfare of the city (Jer 29:7).[17] These spaces for discussion also prevent the vacuum that is often filled by partisan ideologies, helping Christians avoid being discipled by the news cycle or social media. Instead, they learn to be discipled by Jesus and communicate the gospel in civic engagement, public presence, word, and action.

Equipping Christians for public life requires intentional action. Vocational groups, such as gatherings for healthcare workers, tradespeople, laborers, educators, or lawyers, can create an environment where believers discuss how to integrate Christ's lordship into their daily work. These

17. See, e.g., Sandel, *Justice*; Wolterstorff, *Justice*; and compendiums on Catholic Social Teaching such as Pontifical Council for Justice and Peace, *Compendium of the Social Doctrine of the Church.*

gatherings empower individuals to live out their faith in the public sphere, influencing their spheres of influence for justice, mercy, and truth.

Our political actions, convictions, and theologies must reflect our apprenticeship to Jesus and our commitment to his love and mission. This truth raises many questions. How can we allow discipleship and apprenticeship to Jesus to shape our political engagements? How can we apply Jesus's narratives and teachings about God and the kingdom as we seek to engage with the political realities around us? We are apprentices to Jesus. He helps us understand who God is and who we are as God's children. In turn, God calls those of us who are Christian leaders to help people in our churches become full disciples of Jesus Christ: this includes their political actions, convictions, and theologies.

The goal isn't just for Christians to vote or act in the world, but to do so as those whose allegiance belongs to Jesus and his kingdom first. Thus, the church's responsibility to disciple believers for the public square is urgent. This shift from personal morality to public action fosters a robust Christian identity that challenges the world's idols.

SEEKING THE COMMON GOOD, NOT CONTROL

The temptation to impose Christian values through political power has long been a threat to the integrity of the gospel, and yet, Christ calls us to a different path. The Way of Jesus is one of service, love, and advocacy for the common good. The call to pursue the common good isn't a passive stance; it's an active, outward-focused expression of Christ's love for the world.

The church is meant to be a force of peace and reconciliation in the public square, not through coercion or dominance, but through faithful presence and acts of love. Instead of asking, "How can we make our nation Christian?" we must ask, "How can we, as Christians, bless our nation and neighbors?" This posture frees Christians from the idol of control that often dominates political thought. It reorients the believer's mission toward service and advocacy, focusing on issues like poverty, racial reconciliation, family stability, and caring for creation. These are not partisan agendas but kingdom values that reflect God's heart for all people.

We look to Scripture for guidance. Jeremiah 29:7 calls believers to "seek the peace and prosperity of the city" as a way of embodying the kingdom on earth.[18] Early Christians understood this deeply; when plagues

18. Jeremiah 29:7, often cited in discussions of public theology and social engagement; see also Wright, *Surprised by Hope*.

ravaged cities, they cared for all the sick, not just their own.[19] This radical generosity demonstrated their allegiance to Christ and his kingdom, not to the empires that ruled their lands. Similarly, modern Christians can reject a culture war mentality and instead embrace practical, tangible service to their communities. A church might engage in local education, provide job training, or help relieve the burdens of debt for those who are struggling. These and similar actions serve the common good rather than asserting control.

Our call to discipleship includes a political dimension. This includes the need to uphold, engage, and confront the political dynamics and processes of our day and society. We can't avoid this.

The church practices its politics. Our actions are louder than our words. So, what are the political practices of the people of Christ that contribute to the common good? As Christians, we practice our politics in ways that are deeply intertwined with our faith and the teachings of Jesus. At the heart of our political engagement is a commitment to peacemaking and reconciliation, which compels us to confront the principalities and powers that perpetuate injustice and division. We stand with the working class, advocating for those left behind by globalization, technology, and social change. We also speak up for migrants and those who live in constant fear of deportation. Loving our enemies and seeking reconciliation isn't just an abstract idea for us; it's a practice that leads us to embrace the "other" and to build bridges across divides. Proclaiming the gospel is more than just words for us; it's seen in how we break bread, baptize believers, and offer forgiveness.[20]

For us, the kingdom of God isn't merely something we speak of; it's something we live. We announce the kingdom through signs and deeds, advocating for Indigenous rights, caring for orphans and widows, and ensuring that those in need are supported. We believe in sharing power, serving others, and practicing corporate discipline and discernment within our communities. We practice radical hospitality by eating together, opening our homes, and welcoming others into our lives and churches. This is how we bless our neighborhoods and build genuine community. Through our embrace, welcome, and the Beatitudes, we are called to place-making, shaping the spaces we inhabit into communities of peace and love.

19. Stark, *Rise of Christianity.*

20. I've adapted much of this section of this chapter from my post here: Hill, "Engaging Politics as Christians."

God calls us to transcend social, national, political, and cultural barriers, releasing the whole body of Christ to mission and ministry. Our advocacy for the poor and powerless isn't just a political stance; it's the outworking of our love for the silenced, the vulnerable, and the oppressed. We continually examine our associations with power and privilege, asking, "Who is my neighbor?" and responding with courage and compassion. We support marginalized communities as they develop their expressions of faith, knowing that in doing so, we deepen our understanding of Christ and the gospel. We create spaces where values like hospitality, peacemaking, and contemplative-active spirituality shape the way we interact with one another and the world.

We take the scriptural call for mercy, justice, and freedom seriously, engaging critically with the humanities, sciences, economics, and theology as we form our political positions. Our political theology is holistic, encompassing a wide range of topics, from globalization and mission to liberation, hospitality, eco-theology, and ethics. We stand firm in defending freedom of religion, ensuring that everyone has the right to worship without fear. We support policies that promote family stability, seeing it as the foundation for a healthy society. We also prioritize the sanctity of life, advocating for the unborn and defending the dignity of all people. In the same breath, we believe in national security, supporting policies that strengthen society while respecting the dignity of immigrants.

At the heart of our politics is a deep commitment to justice, which compels us to ensure fair elections and to support policies that strike a balance between environmental care and community needs. We champion local businesses to promote economic independence and community flourishing, while fostering a culture of respect for law and order. All children deserve a strong education, especially those in communities that have been left behind. We advocate for policies that equip them with the tools to succeed. Finally, we encourage self-sufficiency and personal responsibility, knowing that a just society must prioritize the well-being of every individual, empowering them to live fully into their calling as image-bearers of God.

I've listed many political practices here. Christians augment these political actions through voting. We choose to witness to Christ through these political actions. And we witness to Jesus through our engagement in "party politics" (both individually and corporately).

Our voting needs to show concern for the issues I have raised above (these include peacemaking, justice, compassion, truth, generosity, etc.).

But, more importantly, we should orient the whole of our lives so that they reflect the mind and passion of Christ in these matters. We do this individually and corporately.

The Micah Network reminds us that we shape political actions and theologies around the biblical vision of abundant life.[21] This includes addressing poverty, corruption, and injustice. But it's also about helping people reach their full potential in all areas of life.

According to Micah, there are fundamental pillars of a more just, peaceful, and sustainable world. This is a world where people can flourish and experience a life of abundance. These pillars are: (1) Economies that are productive, fair, and inclusive. (2) Governments and authorities that are accountable. These must also be responsive to the needs and rights of the poorest and most vulnerable groups. (3) Communities and societies with personal security and without violent conflict. (4) Ecologies that are healthy and that support sustainable flourishing for human beings and other creatures.[22]

As Christians, we believe that human beings find abundant life in a relationship with Jesus Christ and communion with his people.

The common good isn't about securing a Christian monopoly on political power, but about humbling ourselves to serve, to witness, and to advocate for justice. This is how we embody the alternative to nationalism that Christ exemplified: a humble, sacrificial love that transforms the world. Rather than seeking domination or coercive influence, the church's task is to be a witness of love and justice, pointing to a kingdom where Christ reigns over all. As Miroslav Volf writes in *A Public Faith*, the church is called to be a creative force for good, neither withdrawing from society nor seeking to rule over it, but living faithfully within it.[23]

May we refuse the seduction of lesser thrones, standing instead with Jesus Christ, who overturns empires of greed and fear until God in divine holiness, joy, and love alone reigns forever.

21. Micah Global, "Micah Global Resources."

22. Paraphrased from Micah Australia, *Poverty and Biblical Justice*, 7 (no longer available online).

23. Volf, *Public Faith*.

Conclusion: A Dangerous Hope

We've traced shadows and light across the panoramas of nation and soul, listening for the heartbeat of a kingdom made not by human hands but by a holy, eternal God of love. Now, as we stand at the threshold, God's grace invites us to step forward and live as citizens of a realm where mercy reigns and every tear is held.

REVISITING THE CHOICE BETWEEN KINGDOM AND EMPIRE

Arriving at the end of the reflections in this book, we find ourselves once more before the book's first, fiercest question: kingdom or empire? It's no abstract puzzle but a living fork in the road, demanding our deepest convictions, allegiance, and loyalty. We remember crosses hoisted alongside flags in frenzied crowds, remember scripture twisted into swords of exclusion, remember how easy it is to baptize power in the name of Christ and so lose the heart of Jesus's gospel.[1] The question is urgent, raw, and local: Will we pledge ourselves to the cruciform way of Jesus or bow to the glittering illusions of empire?

Jesus said plainly, "My kingdom isn't of this world." Do we believe him? Or does our commitment to our nation and political convictions close our ears to his startling, world-transforming declaration? Jesus's claim that his kingdom isn't of this world isn't an excuse to withdraw into safe piety or political passivity; it's a thunderclap that shatters all worldly pretensions to divine authority.[2] If his kingdom isn't of this world, then no nation, no

1. Cavanaugh, *Migrations of the Holy*, explores how easily Christianity is co-opted by nationalist or state power.

2. Compare John 18:36. See Hauerwas and Willimon, *Resident Aliens*, on the disruptive implications of Jesus's kingdom not being "of this world."

ideology, no president, no prime minister, no ruler, no flag, no political party, no banner, and no constitution can ever lay rightful claim to God's throne and our complete allegiance.

Jesus Christ is the King of kings and the Lord of lords, and his kingdom is supreme over all nations and empires. Only Jesus can command our full loyalty, obedience, sacrifice, and love. Here lies the stark truth that shook Rome to its core: if Jesus is Lord, then Caesar is not (this truth must continue to rock modern empires and nations to their core, too).[3] The early Christians knew this truth in their bones; they gathered in shadowed rooms and whispered prayers that defied the emperor's decrees, staking their very lives on a kingdom without swords or borders, built instead on mercy, truth, humility, righteousness, faith, hope, justice, and fearless love.[4]

And so, the choice stands before us as it did before them. Will we cast our lot with the humble reign of God, or with the restless powers of this age that promise safety yet trade in fear, that preach unity yet breed division? We can't hold both. To follow Jesus is to refuse the throne of domination, to renounce violence masked as righteousness, and to see beyond the shallow triumphs of national pride. It means to stand sometimes painfully apart, to bear witness to a kingdom where people experiencing poverty are lifted, the stranger is welcomed, and the mighty are brought low by the gentle subversion of grace.

This is no hour for half-measures or polite neutrality. The stakes are nothing less than the shape of our souls and the witness of Christ's body on earth. May we have the courage to declare with quiet conviction and burning hearts: our allegiance is to Jesus alone. All else must kneel before that dangerous, liberating claim.

LESSONS TO LIGHT THE WAY

Through these pages, we've traced a fierce and narrow path where the kingdom of God stands in contrast to the empires of this world. We've seen how Jesus revealed a reign not of violence, coercion, fear, exclusion, or national pride but of startling humility, justice, love, inclusion, and reconciling love. From the Sermon on the Mount's beatitudes to the early church's costly confession that "Jesus is Lord," we've learned that no empire can ever rightly

3. A phrase reflecting early church confession against Rome; see Wright, *Paul and the Faithfulness of God*, on "Jesus is Lord, Caesar is not."

4. Kreider, *Patient Ferment of the Early Church*.

claim divine favor, for God's kingdom is forever beyond the grasp of flags, walls, borders, and thrones.

History has served as both a warning and a spotlight. We've watched the church under Nazi Germany and apartheid South Africa fold itself into empire's embrace, baptizing sin, abuse, and cruelty in Christ's name.[5] Yet we've also glimpsed holy defiance: the Confessing Church standing against Hitler's tyranny, believers in South Sudan and Rwanda risking all for peace, and even congregations in the United States of America daring to confront Christian nationalism today.[6] These stories testify that when Christians cling to power, they betray the cross of Jesus Christ. But when we cling to Christ, abiding in the vine, the world is startled awake by a radical love that resists, prophesies, subverts, disarms, and transforms.

So, what wisdom have we gleaned to guide our way? Perhaps it's this: no ruler or nation can sit upon God's throne, the church's true power is found not in seizing influence but in embodying cruciform love, and countless saints before us have chosen the kingdom's narrow, sacrificial, humble, God-glorifying road over the broad avenues and deceptive overtures of empires. Here lies our courage. Here beats our hope. Here displays our love and integrity. That whenever we refuse to wield faith as a weapon, whenever we dismantle walls of hostility, whenever we love our enemies, whenever we welcome the stranger and care for the least, there the kingdom breaks through, iridescent with divine possibility and eternal hope.

We mustn't let these lessons rest idle in our minds but ignite our hearts. To pray "thy kingdom come" is to pledge ourselves to lives of mercy, justice, radical hospitality, and complete allegiance only to Jesus Christ and God's kingdom. May we be found among those who, in resisting the lures of earthly dominion, dare instead to shape communities of peace, bearing witness to a reign that no empire can topple. In such living, the gospel shines undimmed, and the world catches a glimpse of God's new creation dawning among us: the fruit of the life, death, and resurrection of our Lord Jesus Christ.

5. See Confessing Church opposition to Hitler in the *Barmen Declaration* (1934) and South African churches' resistance documented in the *Belhar Confession* (1986).

6. Chapman, *Barmen Theological Declaration*.

THE SPIRIT'S CALL TO PERSONAL AND COMMUNAL TRANSFORMATION

God calls us to personal and communal transformation in every area of our lives, including our civic and political engagements. The reality that "Jesus Christ is Lord" must penetrate deeply into our hearts, shaping how we live, love, contrast, and engage with the world. Acknowledging Christ's lordship is much more than a theological assent. Saying "Jesus Christ is Lord" is both a conviction and a commitment that must lead to practical change, starting within our souls and flowing outward into our communities.[7]

Please make some time to take an honest inventory of your heart. Reflect on where nationalism, political loyalties, populist arguments, or cultural idols have crept in. Are there biases or fears that need to be surrendered to Christ? Do we need to let go of past allegiances, both personal and political, that have shaped our worldview more than the gospel has? The path of transformation isn't always easy, especially when we challenge long-held attitudes or the prevailing narratives within our communities. But it's precisely in moments of difficulty that the Holy Spirit empowers us to change, and Christ Jesus leads us in his narrow way along the path of truth and light.

On a communal level, Jesus calls his church to be a space of radical renewal and grace. Change isn't limited to individuals; it must also extend to the community. This means initiating gracious conversations within the church about the implications of Christ's lordship on our public lives, political views, and civic presence. We may do things like starting a weekly prayer gathering for global peace, advocating for justice in a local community, or learning from marginalized voices. These aren't just actions; they're declarations of allegiance to Christ and his kingdom.

When we, as a body, submit ourselves to his loving, holy, matchless rule and reign, we not only affect our personal lives but also bear witness to the world around us. Genuine, thoroughgoing transformation takes root within the hearts of individuals and the life of the gathered and scattered faith community. As we live differently, beginning with repentance and renewal, we shape the world around us to reflect God's kingdom of justice, faith, hope, love, and grace.

7. Compare Wright, *Simply Jesus*, 175–79, on allegiance to Jesus redefining public and private life.

PROPHETIC ENGAGEMENT WITH THE WORLD

Having been transformed internally, the next step is to engage the world from a place of prophetic clarity. The choice between kingdom and empire doesn't mean disengaging from society. Our decision to give our allegiance to Christ and his kingdom means we must embrace a different form of engagement. We mustn't withdraw from politics or society, but engage with them through the lens of Christ's kingdom, always with a prophetic, humble, redemptive, Christlike posture. The Spirit allows us to love aspects of our country, not by unquestioningly endorsing our nation and its leaders, but by challenging them to live up to the standards of justice, mercy, compassion, and truth that Christ's reign demands.[8]

This kind of engagement doesn't require us to choose sides in the polarized political arenas. Instead, the Spirit empowers us to speak the truth in love, no matter the cost, to both conservatives and progressives, regardless of left and right politics, and everything in between. Our ultimate allegiance is to Christ, and this informs our actions in every sphere of life. The values of Christ's kingdom shape our politics: justice, peace, mercy, and love. God calls us to care for immigrants and refugees, stand against racial and gender injustice, advocate for life, honor and listen to the voices of all socioeconomic classes, work toward peace instead of war, and promote the cause of working-class peoples who struggle to make a living thanks to technologies, trade agreements, and globalization. These actions flow not from a desire to dominate but from a profound commitment to serve the common good.[9]

The prophetic voice of the church must also be one of courage and conviction, especially when our actions don't align with the dominant ideologies of our time. It may mean that we are misunderstood or mischaracterized by others. Jesus told his followers they'd suffer persecutions, beatings, insults, false accusations, imprisonments, hardships, and, often, poverty. However, as Christians, we can expect that this prophetic stance will frequently be liberating, joyous, and countercultural, just as it was in the early church, when believers remained faithful even in the face of persecution.[10] We may not always fit neatly into any political party or cultural

8. Volf, *Public Faith.*

9. For examples and biblical/theological grounding, see Wolterstorff, *Justice*, 270–80.

10. See Kreider, *Patient Ferment of the Early Church*, on early Christian joy and suffering under persecution.

movement, and that is precisely where we need to be, for the church's message of repentance, truth, justice, and grace transcends earthly powers.

As we witness to Christ's lordship, we invite others into a way of life that isn't defined by the ways of the world but by the love and justice of God. This is the gospel in action: a living witness that declares, "Jesus Christ is Lord and he will reign forever," not just in words, but in the way we live, work, and interact with others.

God's call to engage the world prophetically doesn't invite us to a place of comfort, but rather to a place of radical obedience and conformity to Christ. Our actions, words, values, ethics, and lives must demonstrate to the world that Jesus is Lord and that his kingdom has come. We don't show this magnificent, cosmos-defining reality through domination or control, but through self-giving love, humility, and service. This engagement requires courage, but it's a courageous love that always seeks the welfare of others, even when it costs us our own. And it is through this love, this faithful witness, that we bring glory to God and invite others into the hope and peace of Christ's upside-down, joyous, eternal kingdom, which reigns over all empires, just as Jesus Christ reigns supreme over all rulers and powers.

HOPE AND BENEDICTION

As followers of Jesus, we have an unwavering hope, anchored in the sovereignty of God and Christ's ultimate victory. The trials we face in standing for the kingdom of God, the sacrifices we make in the name of truth and justice, aren't in vain. Revelation 11:15 reminds us, "The kingdom of the world has become the kingdom of our Lord and of Christ," a declaration that assures us that every empire, every power, and every system will eventually bow before the Lord. The kingdoms of this world are fleeting, but the kingdom and word of God stand forever.

As we walk this path, we aren't alone. Jesus walks with us every step of the way. His promise remains true: "I am with you always, to the end of the age" (Matt 28:20). Amid uncertainty and opposition, we aren't abandoned, for Christ's presence is a constant source of strength. And we are surrounded by the global community of believers, fellow pilgrims on the same journey, united in the same hope, striving together to bring about the kingdom on earth.

With this hope in our hearts, our Lord Jesus Christ calls us to walk forward with courage, choosing each day the way of the kingdom over the way of empire. It may seem slow, it may seem hard, but we walk in the assurance that justice will prevail, and Christ will be all in all (1 Cor 15:28). His truth, love, and kingdom are eternal, and we are privileged to be a part of this glorious movement.

In this hope, we stand and walk on, choosing, each day, the way of the kingdom over the way of empire, until that day when God's will is done on earth as it is in heaven. Let this be our prayer, our calling, and our joy.

So, let's step into the world with hearts set aflame, daring to trust that God's kingdom of mercy and justice will rise (even amid the rubble of our failed empires) and reign forever. When darkness gathers thick, may God's Spirit assure you that even the tiniest ember of Christ's light can shatter the night. Hope isn't naïve. Our faith, hope, and love are defiance against despair, anchored in the promise that the cross of Christ and the love of God will have the final word.[11] Now is the hour to stand unflinching, to break allegiance with idols, and to embody the fierce compassion of Jesus, becoming the hands that heal, the voices that speak truth to power, and the feet that carry good news into every wounded place.

11. Wright, *Surprised by Hope*.

Appendix: Reflection Questions for Individuals and Groups

INTRODUCTION: WHEN THE CROSS IS CAPTURED

1. Where have I seen the cross of Christ "captured" by political or cultural forces in my context, and how might God be inviting me to resist this distortion?
2. How does the contrast between Jesus's kingdom and today's empires challenge the ways I live out my faith in public and private life?

CHAPTER 1: KINGDOM OR EMPIRE? JESUS'S VISION IN AN AGE OF POLITICAL POWER

1. How does Jesus's vision of the kingdom disrupt my assumptions about power, success, and influence?
2. In what ways might I need to shift my allegiance from the empires of this world to the radical, self-giving reign of God?

CHAPTER 2: CHRISTIAN NATIONALISM AND THE SEDUCTION OF POWER

1. Where do I see Christian nationalism tempting the church (or myself) to equate God's kingdom with national interests or identity?

2. What practical steps can I take to disentangle my discipleship from unhealthy nationalistic loyalties?

CHAPTER 3: POPULISM AND THE PEOPLE OF GOD

1. How does populist rhetoric appeal to my fears or biases, and how might Jesus be calling me to a deeper trust in his way of love and justice?
2. What does it look like to remain grounded in the kingdom of God when public movements demand simple answers and emotional loyalty?

CHAPTER 4: THE CROSS IN HITLER'S SHADOW

1. What can I learn from the Confessing Church's resistance to Nazi ideology about courageously maintaining gospel faithfulness today?
2. Where might I be tempted to stay silent in the face of injustice, and what would it mean to bear the cost of discipleship in my context?

CHAPTER 5: APARTHEID AND THE BODY OF CHRIST

1. How does the church's complicity and resistance during apartheid challenge me to examine racial injustice and segregation today?
2. What does genuine reconciliation and solidarity with the oppressed look like in my life and community?

CHAPTER 6: KINGDOM CITIZENS IN PUBLIC LIFE

1. How can I faithfully participate in public life (politics, economics, culture) while keeping my deepest loyalty to Christ's kingdom?
2. What practices help me discern when my engagement in public life starts to mirror the empire more than the kingdom?

CHAPTER 7: THE CROSS AND THE FLAG

1. When have I witnessed (or participated in) blending national symbols with the gospel in ways that compromise Christ's message?
2. How might I reclaim the cross as a symbol of sacrificial love and hope, rather than political triumph or identity?

CHAPTER 8: JESUS IS LORD

1. What does it mean for me to declare, "Jesus is Lord" in a culture where many other powers demand my allegiance?
2. Where do I need to realign my life, habits, or relationships so they reflect Jesus's lordship above all else?

CONCLUSION: A DANGEROUS HOPE

1. How does embracing the hope of God's kingdom empower me to live courageously and prophetically in an age of fear and division?
2. What specific, risky acts of love, justice, or reconciliation might this hope be calling me to embody right now?

About the Author

Graham Joseph Hill (OAM, PhD) is an Adjunct Research Fellow and Associate Professor at Charles Sturt University and one of Australia's most prolific and awarded Christian authors. He's written more than twenty books, including *Salt, Light, and a City*, which was named Jesus Creed's 2012 Book of the Year (church category); *Healing Our Broken Humanity* (with Grace Ji-Sun Kim), named Outreach Magazine's 2019 Resource of the Year (culture category); and *World Christianity*, shortlisted for the 2025 Australian Christian Book of the Year. In 2024, Graham was awarded the Medal of the Order of Australia (OAM) for his service to theological education. He lives in Sydney with his wife, Shyn.

See Graham's author website and Substack:
grahamjosephhill.com
grahamjosephhill.substack.com

Bibliography

The AND Campaign. *Compassion (&) Conviction: The AND Campaign's Guide to Faithful Civic Engagement.* Downers Grove, IL: InterVarsity, 2020.

Ashworth, John. *The Voice of the Voiceless: The Role of the Church in the Sudanese Civil War.* Nairobi: Paulines Africa, 2014.

Augustine. *The City of God.* Translated by Henry Bettenson. London: Penguin, 1972.

Baptist Joint Committee for Religious Liberty (BJC) and the Freedom From Religion Foundation (FFRF). "Christian Nationalism and the January 6, 2021 Insurrection." BJC, February 9, 2022. https://bjconline.org/jan6report/.

The Barmen Theological Declaration (1934). In *Documents of the Christian Church,* edited by Henry Bettenson and Chris Maunder, 388–90. Oxford: Oxford University Press, 2011.

Barnett, Victoria. *For the Soul of the People: Protestant Protest Against Hitler.* New York: Oxford University Press, 1992.

The Belhar Confession. September 1986; online May 2020. https://vialogue.wordpress.com/wp-content/uploads/2020/05/belharconfession.pdf.

The Belhar Confession. Dutch Reformed Mission Church, South Africa, 1986.

Bellah, Robert N. "Civil Religion in America." *Daedalus* 96 (1967) 1–21.

Belmonte, Kevin. *William Wilberforce: A Hero for Humanity.* New York: HarperCollins, 2007.

Bergen, Doris L. *Twisted Cross: The German Christian Movement in the Third Reich.* Chapel Hill: University of North Carolina Press, 1996.

Bethge, Eberhard. *Dietrich Bonhoeffer: A Biography.* Minneapolis: Fortress, 2000.

Bettenson, Henry, and Chris Maunder, eds. *Documents of the Christian Church.* Oxford: Oxford University Press, 2011.

Bock, Darrell, ed. *The Cape Town Commitment: A Confession of Faith and a Call to Action.* Eugene, OR: Wipf & Stock, 2013.

Boesak, Allan, and Curtiss Paul DeYoung. *Radical Reconciliation: Beyond Political Pietism and Christian Quietism.* Maryknoll, NY: Orbis, 2012.

Bonhoeffer, Dietrich. *The Cost of Discipleship.* Translated by R. H. Fuller. New York: Macmillan, 1957.

———. *Discipleship.* Translated by Barbara Green and Reinhard Krauss. Minneapolis: Fortress, 2015.

———. *Ethics.* New York: Touchstone, 1995.

———. *Letters and Papers from Prison.* Edited by Eberhard Bethge. New York: Touchstone, 1997.

———. *Life Together*. Translated by John W. Doberstein. Norwich: SCM, 1954.

Bosch, David J. *Transforming Mission: Paradigm Shifts in Theology of Mission*. Maryknoll, NY: Orbis, 2011.

Boyd, Gregory A. *The Myth of a Christian Nation: How the Quest for Political Power Is Destroying the Church*. Grand Rapids: Zondervan, 2006.

Brueggemann, Walter. *Isaiah 1–39*. Louisville, KY: Westminster John Knox, 1998.

———. *The Prophetic Imagination*. Minneapolis: Fortress, 2001.

———. *Theology of the Old Testament: Testimony, Dispute, Advocacy*. Minneapolis: Fortress, 2012.

Busch, Eberhard. *The Barmen Theses Then and Now*. Grand Rapids: Eerdmans, 2010.

Butler, Anthea. *White Evangelical Racism: The Politics of Morality in America*. Chapel Hill: The University of North Carolina Press, 2012.

Cavanaugh, William T. *Migrations of the Holy: God, State, and the Political Meaning of the Church*. Grand Rapids: Eerdmans, 2011.

Chaggaris, Steve. "Elizabeth Warren: 'The System Is Rigged.'" *CBS News*, September 6, 2012. https://www.cbsnews.com/news/elizabeth-warren-the-system-is-rigged/.

Chapman, Peter, trans. *Barmen Theological Declaration*. May 29–31, 1934. https://creedsandconfessions.org/barmen-declaration.html.

Christians for Social Action. "Our Mission and Vision." https://christiansforsocialaction.org.

Compier, Don H., et al. *Empire and the Christian Tradition: New Readings of Classical Theologians*. Minneapolis: Fortress, 2007.

Costas, Orlando E. *Christ Outside the Gate: Mission Beyond Christendom*. Maryknoll, NY: Orbis, 1982.

Coyne, Daniel. "Populism and Religion: A Conclusion." London School of Economics, February 12, 2019. https://blogs.lse.ac.uk/religionglobalsociety/2019/02/populism-and-religion-a-conclusion/.

Cremer, Tobias. "The Religion Gap: Why Right-Wing Populists Underperform Among Christian Voters and What This Means for the Role of the Church in Society." London School of Economics, December 20, 2018. https://blogs.lse.ac.uk/religionglobalsociety/2018/12/the-religion-gap-why-right-wing-populists-underperform-among-christian-voters-and-what-this-means-for-the-role-of-the-church-in-society/.

Crossan, John Dominic. *God and Empire: Jesus Against Rome, Then and Now*. San Francisco: HarperOne, 2008.

De Gruchy, John W. *Bonhoeffer and South Africa: Theology in Dialogue*. Grand Rapids: Eerdmans, 1984.

———. *The Church Struggle in South Africa*. Minneapolis: Fortress, 2005.

———. *Reconciliation: Restoring Justice*. Minneapolis: Fortress, 2002.

DeHanas, Daniel Nilsson. "Sacred, Supernatural, and Apocalyptic Populism." London School of Economics, December 17, 2018. https://blogs.lse.ac.uk/religionglobalsociety/2018/12/sacred-supernatural-and-apocalyptic-populism/.

Deverell, Garry Worete. *Gondwana Theology: A Trawloolway Man Reflects on Christian Faith*. Melbourne: Morning Star, 2018.

Dias, Elizabeth, and Ruth Graham. "How White Evangelicals Fused with Trump Extremism." *New York Times*, January 11, 2021. https://www.nytimes.com/2021/01/11/us/how-white-evangelical-christians-fused-with-trump-extremism.html.

Du Mez, Kristin Kobes. *Jesus and John Wayne: How White Evangelicals Corrupted a Faith and Fractured a Nation*. New York: Norton, 2020.

Dussel, Enrique. *A History of the Church in Latin America: Colonialism to Liberation (1492–1979)*. Grand Rapids: Eerdmans, 1981.

Ehrman, Bart D., ed. *The Apostolic Fathers*. Vol. 1: *I Clement, II Clement, Ignatius, Polycarp, Didache*. Loeb Classical Library 24. Cambridge, MA: Harvard University Press, 2003.

Ellul, Jacques. *The Humiliation of the Word*. Grand Rapids: Eerdmans, 1985.

———. *The Presence of the Kingdom*. Colorado Springs: Helmers & Howard, 1989.

The Epistle to Diognetus. In *The Apostolic Fathers*, edited and translated by Bart D. Ehrman, 2:130–59. Loeb Classical Library 25. Cambridge, MA: Harvard University Press, 2003.

Ericksen, Robert P. *Complicity in the Holocaust: Churches and Universities in Nazi Germany*. Cambridge: Cambridge University Press, 2012.

Evangelische Kirche in Deutschland. *Barmer Theologische Erklärung*. https://www.ekd.de/barmer-theologische-erklarung-thesen-11296.htm.

Evans, Richard J. *The Third Reich in Power, 1933–1939*. New York: Penguin, 2006.

Fea, John. *Believe Me: The Evangelical Road to Donald Trump*. Grand Rapids: Eerdmans, 2018.

Foster, Richard. *Celebration of Discipline: The Path to Spiritual Growth*. San Francisco: HarperSanFrancisco, 1988.

Girard, René. *I See Satan Fall Like Lightning*. Translated by James G. Williams. Maryknoll, NY: Orbis, 2001.

Gorman, Michael J. *Becoming the Gospel: Paul, Participation, and Mission*. Grand Rapids: Eerdmans, 2015.

———. *Cruciformity: Paul's Narrative Spirituality of the Cross*. Grand Rapids: Eerdmans, 2001.

———. *Reading Revelation Responsibly: Uncivil Worship and Witness*. Eugene, OR: Cascade, 2011.

Greenleaf, Robert K. *Servant Leadership: A Journey into the Nature of Legitimate Power and Greatness*. New York: Paulist, 1977.

Gumbleton, Thomas John. "Homily at the Beatification of Franz Jägerstätter." *National Catholic Reporter*, October 26, 2007. https://www.ncronline.org/blogs/peace-pulpit/homily-beatification-franz-j-gerst-tter.

Gutiérrez, Gustavo. *A Theology of Liberation: History, Politics, and Salvation*. Maryknoll, NY: Orbis, 1988.

Hallie, Philip P. *Lest Innocent Blood Be Shed: The Story of the Village of Le Chambon and How Goodness Happened There*. New York: HarperPerennial, 1994.

Halsted, Matthew L. "Quote: Epistle to Diognetus." Dr. Matthew L. Halsted (blog), September 13, 2021. https://matthewhalsted.com/2021/09/13/quote-epistle-to-diognetus/.

Hamm, Thomas D. *The Quakers in America*. New York: Columbia University Press, 2003.

Harris, John. *One Blood: 200 Years of Aboriginal Encounter with Christianity*. Sutherland: Albatross, 1990.

Hauerwas, Stanley. *Matthew*. Grand Rapids: Brazos, 2006.

———. *The Peaceable Kingdom: A Primer in Christian Ethics*. Notre Dame, IN: University of Notre Dame Press, 1991.

Hauerwas, Stanley, and William H. Willimon. *Resident Aliens: Life in the Christian Colony*. Nashville: Abingdon, 1989.

Hays, Richard B. *The Moral Vision of the New Testament: Community, Cross, New Creation*. San Francisco: HarperCollins, 1996.

Heschel, Susannah. *The Aryan Jesus: Christian Theologians and the Bible in Nazi Germany*. Princeton: Princeton University Press, 2008.

Hill, Graham Joseph. "A Conversation with Lamin Sanneh on World Christianity, Christian-Muslim Relations, and Translating the Christian Message." GrahamJosephHill.com, December 15, 2023. https://grahamjosephhill.com/lamin-sanneh/.

———. "Engaging Politics as Christians." GrahamJosephHill.com, December 15, 2023. https://grahamjosephhill.com/engaging-politics-as-christians/.

———. "How to Write a Lament." GrahamJosephHill.com, December 15, 2023. https://grahamjosephhill.com/lament/.

———, ed. *Relentless Love: Living Out Integral Mission to Combat Poverty, Injustice, and Conflict*. Carlisle: Langham, 2020.

———. *Ten Movements of the Jesus Way: Shifting from Worldly Self-Interest to Radical Discipleship*. Downers Grove, IL: InterVarsity, 2026.

———. *World Christianity: An Introduction*. Eugene, OR: Cascade, 2024.

Hill, Graham Joseph, and Grace Ji-Sun Kim. *Healing Our Broken Humanity: Practices for Revitalizing the Church and Renewing the World*. Downers Grove, IL: InterVarsity, 2018.

Hillsong Worship. "This I Believe (The Creed)." Track 6 on *No Other Name*. Hillsong Music, 2014.

Hochschild, Arlie Russell. *Strangers in Their Own Land: Anger and Mourning on the American Right*. New York: The New Press, 2016.

Holmes, Michael W., ed. and trans. *The Apostolic Fathers: Greek Texts and English Translations*. 3rd ed. Grand Rapids: Baker Academic, 2007.

Horsley, Richard A. *Jesus and Empire: The Kingdom of God and the New World Disorder*. Minneapolis: Fortress, 2002.

Hunter, James Davison. *To Change the World: The Irony, Tragedy, and Possibility of Christianity in the Late Modern World*. New York: Oxford University Press, 2010.

Hurtado, Larry W. *Destroyer of the Gods: Early Christian Distinctiveness in the Roman World*. Waco, TX: Baylor University Press, 2016.

Interparliamentary Assembly on Orthodoxy. "Statement on the Invasion in Ukraine." February 28, 2022. https://orthodoxeurope.org/news/2022/03/16/declaration-ukraine.

Jeremias, Jörg. *The Book of Amos: A Commentary*. Louisville, KY: Westminster John Knox, 1998.

Johnson, Elizabeth A. *Ask the Beasts: Darwin and the God of Love*. London: Bloomsbury, 2014.

The Kairos Document: Challenge to the Church: A Theological Comment on the Political Crisis in South Africa. Kairos Theologians, September 22, 1985. https://sahistory.org.za/archive/challenge-church-theological-comment-political-crisis-south-africa-kairos-document-1985.

Keller, Catherine. *On the Mystery: Discerning Divinity in Process*. Minneapolis: Fortress, 2007.

Keller, Timothy. *Center Church: Doing Balanced, Gospel-Centered Ministry in Your City*. Grand Rapids: Zondervan, 2012.

King Center. "The Beloved Community." https://thekingcenter.org/about-tkc/the-king-philosophy/.

King, Martin Luther, Jr. "Letter from a Birmingham Jail." April 16, 1963. https://www.africa.upenn.edu/Articles_Gen/Letter_Birmingham.html.

Kreider, Alan. *The Patient Ferment of the Early Church: The Improbable Rise of Christianity in the Roman Empire*. Grand Rapids: Baker Academic, 2016.

Lagerwey, Caleb. "How to End Christian Nationalism." *Reformed Journal*, March 5, 2025. https://reformedjournal.com/2025/03/05/45594/.

Leeman, Jonathan. *How the Nations Rage: Rethinking Faith and Politics in a Divided Age*. Nashville: Thomas Nelson, 2018.

Leonhardt, David, and Arlie Russell Hochschild. "It's Not Just Trump Voters. Both Parties Are in Denial." *New York Times*, *The Opinions* podcast, June 16, 2025. https://podcasts.apple.com/au/podcast/the-opinions/id1762898126?i=1000713068457.

Long, Huey. *Every Man a King: The Autobiography of Huey P. Long*. Chicago: Quadrangle, 1964.

Longman, Timothy. *Christianity and Genocide in Rwanda*. New York: Cambridge University Press, 2010.

Luchenko, Ksenia. "Why the Russian Orthodox Church Supports the War in Ukraine." *Carnegie Politika*, January 31, 2023. https://carnegieendowment.org/russia-eurasia/politika/2023/01/why-the-russian-orthodox-church-supports-the-war-in-ukraine.

Main, Thomas J. *The Rise of Illiberalism*. Dublin: Bloomsbury, 2022.

Mandaville, Peter. *The Geopolitics of Religious Soft Power: How States Use Religion in Foreign Policy*. Oxford: Oxford University Press, 2023.

The Martyrdom of Polycarp. In *The Apostolic Fathers: Greek Texts and English Translations*, edited and translated by Michael W. Holmes, 306–27. Grand Rapids: Baker Academic, 2007.

Marzouki, Nadia, et al., eds. *Saving the People: How Populists Hijack Religion*. Oxford: Oxford University Press, 2016.

McDade, Stefani. "N.T. Wright: What Jesus Would Say to the 'Empire' Today." *Christianity Today*, August 14, 2024. https://www.christianitytoday.com/2024/08/nt-wright-mike-bird-jesus-powers-christians-politics-2024/.

McKnight, Scot. *Kingdom Conspiracy: Returning to the Radical Mission of the Local Church*. Grand Rapids: Brazos, 2016.

Micah Australia. *Poverty and Biblical Justice*. Sydney: Micah Australia, 2016.

Micah Global. "Micah Global Resources." https://micahglobal.org/page/resources-external.

Miller, Paul D. *The Religion of American Greatness: What's Wrong with Christian Nationalism*. Downers Grove, IL: IVP Academic, 2022.

Moltmann, Jürgen. *God in Creation: A New Theology of Creation and the Spirit of God*. Minneapolis: Augsburg Fortress, 1993.

Moo, Douglas J. *The Letter of James*. Grand Rapids: Eerdmans, 2000.

Mouw, Richard J. *Uncommon Decency: Christian Civility in an Uncivil World*. Downers Grove, IL: InterVarsity, 2010.

Mudde, Cas, and Cristóbal Rovira Kaltwasser. *Populism: A Very Short Introduction*. Oxford: Oxford University Press, 2017.

Mulholland, M. Robert, Jr. *Invitation to a Journey: A Road Map for Spiritual Formation*. Downers Grove, IL: InterVarsity, 2016.

Müller, Jan-Werner. *What Is Populism?* Philadelphia: University of Pennsylvania Press, 2016.

Murphy, Nancey, et al. *Virtues and Practices in the Christian Tradition: Christian Ethics After MacIntyre*. Notre Dame, IN: University of Notre Dame Press, 1997.

Newbigin, Lesslie. *The Household of God: Lectures on the Nature of the Church*. London: SCM, 1953.

"The Nicene Creed, 325." In *Documents of the Christian Church*, edited by Henry Bettenson and Chris Maunder, 58–59. Oxford: Oxford University Press, 2011.

Nicols, John. "Bernie Sanders Readies a 'Which Side Are You On?' Presidential Bid." *The Nation*, April 29, 2015. https://www.thenation.com/article/archive/bernie-sanders-readies-which-side-are-you-presidential-bid/.

Norris, Pippa, and Ronald Inglehart. *Cultural Backlash: Trump, Brexit, and Authoritarian Populism*. New York: Cambridge University Press, 2019.

Nouwen, Henri J. M. *Reaching Out: The Three Movements of the Spiritual Life*. Garden City, NY: Doubleday, 1975.

———. *The Wounded Healer: Ministry in Contemporary Society*. New York: Image, 1979.

O'Donovan, Oliver. *The Desire of the Nations: Rediscovering the Roots of Political Theology*. Cambridge: Cambridge University Press, 2008.

O'Malley, Brian Patrick. "Under God: Understanding Its Revolutionary Usage." *Journal of the American Revolution*, July 22, 2019. https://allthingsliberty.com/2019/07/under-god-understanding-its-revolutionary-usage/.

Osborne, Grant. "John 6:15." Verse-by-Verse Commentary, April 7, 2017. https://versebyversecommentary.com/2017/04/07/john-615/.

Palin, Sarah. "Speech at the Republican National Convention." September 3, 2008. Transcript via NPR. https://www.npr.org/2008/09/03/94258995/transcript-gov-sarah-palin-at-the-rnc.

Pattel-Gray, Anne. *Through Aboriginal Eyes: The Cry from the Wilderness*. Geneva: WCC, 1991.

Peppiatt, Lucy. *The Imago Dei: Humanity Made in the Image of God*. Eugene, OR: Cascade, 2022.

Peterson, Eugene H. *Christ Plays in Ten Thousand Places: A Conversation in Spiritual Theology*. Grand Rapids: Eerdmans, 2005.

———. *A Long Obedience in the Same Direction: Discipleship in an Instant Society*. Downers Grove, IL: InterVarsity, 2021.

Pillay, Gerald John. *Religion at the Limits? Pentecostalism Among Indian South Africans*. Pretoria: University of South Africa Press, 1994.

Pontifical Council for Justice and Peace. *Compendium of the Social Doctrine of the Church*. Vatican City: Libreria Editrice Vaticana, 2004.

Putnam, Robert D., and David E. Campbell. *American Grace: How Religion Divides and Unites Us*. New York: Simon & Schuster, 2010.

Reagan, Ronald. "A Vision for America." Speech to the Republican National Convention, July 17, 1980. American Rhetoric. https://www.americanrhetoric.com/speeches/ronaldreagan1980rnc.htm.

Reed, Erik. "Jesus Is Lord, Caesar Is Not." *WORLD*, August 31, 2022. https://wng.org/opinions/jesus-is-lord-caesar-is-not-1661946872.

Rieger, Joerg. *Jesus vs. Caesar: For People Tired of Serving the Wrong God*. Nashville: Abingdon, 2018.

Roy, Olivier. "A Kitsch Christianity: Populists Gather Support While Traditional Religiosity Declines." London School of Economics, October 22, 2018. https://blogs.

lse.ac.uk/religionglobalsociety/2018/10/a-kitsch-christianity-populists-gather-support-while-traditional-religiosity-declines/.

Ryan, Ben. "Christianism: A Crude Political Ideology and the Triumph of Empty Symbolism." London School of Economics, November 5, 2018. https://blogs.lse.ac.uk/religionglobalsociety/2018/11/christianism-a-crude-political-ideology-and-the-triumph-of-empty-symbolism/.

Sandel, Michael J. *Justice: What's the Right Thing to Do?* New York: Farrar, Straus and Giroux, 2009.

Sanneh, Lamin. *Whose Religion Is Christianity? The Gospel Beyond the West.* Grand Rapids: Eerdmans, 2004.

Schaff, Philip, ed. *The Creeds of Christendom.* Vol. 2. New York: Harper & Brothers, 1877.

Scholl, Inge. *The White Rose: Munich 1942–1943.* Middletown, CT: Wesleyan University Press, 1983.

Smith, James K. A. *Desiring the Kingdom: Worship, Worldview, and Cultural Formation.* Grand Rapids: Baker Academic, 2009.

Sobrino, Jon. *Jesus the Liberator: A Historical-Theological Reading of Jesus of Nazareth.* Maryknoll, NY: Orbis, 1996.

Sölle, Dorothee. *The Silent Cry: Mysticism and Resistance.* Minneapolis: Fortress, 2001.

Spencer, Nick. "The Rise of Christian Populism." Bible Society, October 6, 2017. https://www.biblesociety.org.uk/latest/news/the-rise-of-christian-populism.

———. "The Rise of Christian Populism." *Theos*, January 7, 2021. https://www.theosthinktank.co.uk/comment/2021/01/07/the-rise-of-christian-populism.

Stark, Rodney. *The Rise of Christianity: How the Obscure, Marginal Jesus Movement Became the Dominant Religious Force in the Western World in a Few Centuries.* San Francisco: HarperCollins, 1997.

Stooksberry, Jay. "Us-Versus-Them: The Pronouns of Populism." *Reason*, November 2, 2024. https://reason.com/2024/11/02/us-versus-them-the-pronouns-of-populism/.

Stott, John R. W. *Basic Christian Leadership: Biblical Models of Church, Gospel and Ministry.* Downers Grove, IL: InterVarsity, 2006.

"Stuttgarter Schuldbekenntnis." In *Kirchliches Jahrbuch für die Evangelische Kirche in Deutschland 1945–1948*, edited by Joachim Beckmann, 438–39. Gütersloh: C. Bertelsmann, 1950.

Swanson, David W. "Christian Nationalism: What Defines It?" Missio Alliance, March 15, 2022. https://www.missioalliance.org/christian-nationalism-what-defines-it/.

———. *Rediscipling the White Church: From Cheap Diversity to True Solidarity.* Downers Grove, IL: InterVarsity, 2020.

Taylor, Jenny J. "Changing the World Through Faithful Presence: A Book Review of 'To Change the World.'" Lausanne Global Analysis, August 2017. https://lausanne.org/global-analysis/changing-world-faithful-presence.

Tertullian. *Apology: De Spectaculis. Minucius Felix: Octavius.* Translated by T. R. Glover and Gerald H. Rendall. Loeb Classical Library 250. Cambridge, MA: Harvard University Press, 1931.

Trump, Donald. "Nomination Acceptance Speech at the Republican National Convention." July 21, 2016. Transcript via Politico. https://www.politico.com/story/2016/07/full-transcript-donald-trump-nomination-acceptance-speech-at-rnc-225974.

Tutu, Desmond. *No Future Without Forgiveness.* New York: Image, 2000.

Tyler, Amanda. *How to End Christian Nationalism.* Minneapolis: Broadleaf, 2024.

Villa-Vicencio, Charles. *The Spirit of Freedom: South African Leaders on Religion and Politics*. Berkeley: University of California Press, 1996.

———. *Trapped in Apartheid: A Socio-Theological History of the English-Speaking Churches*. Maryknoll, NY: Orbis, 1988.

———. *Walk with Us and Listen: Political Reconciliation in Africa*. Washington: Georgetown University Press, 2009.

Volf, Miroslav. *Exclusion and Embrace: A Theological Exploration of Identity, Otherness, and Reconciliation*. Nashville: Abingdon, 1996.

———. *A Public Faith: How Followers of Christ Should Serve the Common Good*. Grand Rapids: Brazos, 2013.

Wehner, Peter. "The Evangelical Church Is Breaking Apart." *The Atlantic*, October 24, 2021. https://www.theatlantic.com/ideas/archive/2021/10/evangelical-church-breaking-apart/620469/.

Wheelock, Eleazar. *Liberty of Conscience; or, No King but Christ, in His Church: A Sermon, Preached at Dartmouth-Hall, November 30th, 1775*. Hartford: Eben Watson, 1776.

Whitehead, Andrew L., and Samuel L. Perry. *Taking America Back for God: Christian Nationalism in the United States*. New York: Oxford University Press, 2020.

Wikipedia. "Make America Great Again." Modified August 27, 2025. https://en.wikipedia.org/wiki/Make_America_Great_Again.

Willard, Dallas. *The Divine Conspiracy: Rediscovering Our Hidden Life in God*. San Francisco: HarperCollins, 1998.

Wolterstorff, Nicholas. *Justice: Rights and Wrongs*. Princeton: Princeton University Press, 2010.

Woodley, Randy. *Shalom and the Community of Creation: An Indigenous Vision*. Grand Rapids: Eerdmans, 2012.

Wright, Christopher J. H. *The Mission of God: Unlocking the Bible's Grand Narrative*. Downers Grove, IL: IVP Academic, 2006.

Wright, N. T. *After You Believe: Why Christian Character Matters*. New York: HarperOne, 2012.

———. *The Day the Revolution Began: Reconsidering the Meaning of Jesus's Crucifixion*. New York: HarperCollins, 2016.

———. "The Early Christians and the Mission of God: The Michael Green Memorial Lecture." N. T. Wright Page, December 9, 2019. https://ntwrightpage.com/2020/03/30/the-early-christians-and-the-mission-of-god-the-michael-green-memorial-lecture/.

———. *How God Became King: The Forgotten Story of the Gospels*. New York: HarperOne, 2012.

———. *Jesus and the Victory of God*. Minneapolis: Fortress, 1997.

———. *The Lord and His Prayer*. London: SPCK, 1996.

———. *The Meal Jesus Gave Us*. Louisville, KY: Westminster John Knox, 2002.

———. *Paul and the Faithfulness of God*. Minneapolis: Fortress 2013.

———. *Paul: In Fresh Perspective*. Minneapolis: Augsburg, 2009.

———. *Simply Jesus: A New Vision of Who He Was, What He Did, and Why He Matters*. New York: HarperOne, 2011.

———. *Surprised by Hope: Rethinking Heaven, the Resurrection, and the Mission of the Church*. New York: HarperOne, 2008.

Zahn, Gordon C. *In Solitary Witness: The Life and Death of Franz Jägerstätter*. New York: Holt, Rinehart and Winston, 1964.

www.ingramcontent.com/pod-product-compliance
Lightning Source LLC
LaVergne TN
LVHW090520110826
845146LV00003B/935

* 9 7 9 8 3 8 5 2 6 2 7 0 0 *